Hugh S

C000002746

A Manual of
Sea Fishing Baits

 Ernest Benn

Hugh Stoker's series of county guides

Sea Fishing in Cornwall
Sea Fishing in North Devon and Somerset
Sea Fishing in South Devon
Sea Fishing in Dorset
Sea Fishing in Hampshire and the Isle of Wight
Sea Fishing in Sussex
Sea Fishing in Kent

Other Benn books by Hugh Stoker

Sea Angling with the Specimen Hunters (Ed.)
Complete Guide to Sea Fishing

Other books in the
Benn Fishing Handbooks Series

The Super Flies of Still Water
John Goddard
Fifty Favourite Nymphs
T. Donald Overfield
Floatmaker's Manual
Bill Watson

Cover photograph reproduced
by courtesy of *Angling Times*

Published by
Ernest Benn Limited
25 New Street Square, London, EC4A 3JA
& Sovereign Way, Tonbridge, Kent, TN9 1RW

First published 1978
© Hugh Stoker 1978

Printed in Great Britain by the Anchor Press, Tiptree, Essex
ISBN 0 510-22517-9

Contents

Part One
Baits from Sand or Muddy Sand

Lugworms

The lugworm *(Arenicola marina)* is one of our most widely used sea angling baits. Large colonies of these burrowing marine worms are found all around the British Isles wherever there is some shelter from wave action and the foreshore consists of firm, gently shelving sand or muddy sand. They are particularly numerous on estuarial tide-flats, and in shallow bays protected from the prevailing westerly winds.

In appearance the lugworm possesses a plump cylindrical body bearing tufts of bristles and gills, terminating in a shorter and thinner tail-section that is usually filled with sand.

Lugworms differ considerably in size, colour and flesh-texture from one stretch of coast to another, depending on the varying nature of their habitat and the nutritional content of the sand. With one notable exception (which we will deal with later) each lugworm lives in its own U-shaped burrow in the sand. Nourishment is obtained from the decaying organic matter contained in its rather uninteresting diet of sand and mud.

Most colonies of lugworm spawn in the autumn, with maximum spawning activity occurring during neap tides between October and December. The egg masses contain thousands of embryos, and the larvae hatch out within four or five days.

Digging
As the foreshore becomes exposed to the ebbing tide, the presence of lugworm is revealed to the bait-digger by the familiar spiral mounds of sandy excrement, known

1

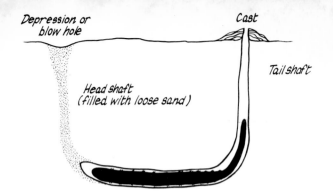

Fig. 1   The lugworm in its burrow. The tail shaft and lower gallery are open, but the head shaft is filled with loose sand which descends slowly from the surface as the lugworm eats into it from below.

as 'casts', which often cover the surface of the damp sand in their thousands. About 6 to 10 inches from each cast there is a corresponding small circular depression in the sand, about the size of a 2p piece, marking the other extremity of the U-shaped burrow. (See Fig. 1.) These are sometimes referred to as 'blow-holes', and for the sake of convenience I'll use the term here.

For much of the time a lugworm lies in its burrow between the cast and the blow-hole, with its head always facing towards the blow-shaft. Usually it will be about a foot below the surface, although the average depth may vary considerably from one bait ground to another.

A broad-tined potato digging fork is the best tool for digging lug where they are found at a reasonably accessible depth, but for deep-burrowing lug (notably the highly-prized large black lugworm) you may need to use a narrow-bladed spade. However, when using a spade one must take extra care to avoid chopping the worms in half.

On most lug grounds the worms are spread out over a fairly wide area between the tide lines, although as a general rule the biggest worms are found well down the beach. The method of digging varies according to local conditions. On a bait ground where the worms are large and fairly thinly scattered it usually saves a lot of hard work if the worms are dug individually. This is done by selecting a likely-looking cast and blow-hole, and then taking out a preliminary forkful of sand close to the blow without actually cutting into the shaft. Next you remove a second forkful of sand near the cast end.

This completes the preliminaries, and all you have to do now is to thrust the fork in to its full depth so that it angles in under the estimated line of the lugworm's burrow. As the laden fork is lifted clear of the hole it should be turned over with a quick flick, causing the lowest layer of sand to finish up near the top of the heap. A careful stirring motion with the flat of the tines should expose the lugworm, which is then transferred into a plastic bucket or bait-box. If the first forkful doesn't produce the worm, go down a bit deeper.

Some bait-diggers try to save time by making a direct attack on the lugworm in its burrow without taking out

Fig. 2   A flat expanse of sheltered sandy foreshore can nearly always be relied upon to yield a rich supply of bait. This fisherman is digging lugworm, but the other baits obtainable in the same area include white ragworm, cockles and (at low spring tides) razorfish.

the two preliminary holes at either end. This may work well enough if the worms are lying very shallow, but normally the extra suction of the "direct attack" method puts a lot of strain on the fork handle – especially when digging deep into a sticky sand/mud mixture.

There's nothing more frustrating than to hear a sudden splintering crack while bait-digging, and to be left clutching a broken fork. Needless to say, this always seems to happen when (a) you are using a borrowed fork and (b) the bait-box is still almost empty!

When lug are abundant it is often difficult to decide which blow-hole belongs to which cast – and then a more rewarding method may be 'patch-digging'. This is best done by opening up a narrow strip of likely-looking sand, then digging backwards from it, using the sand just extracted to fill the strip previously excavated.

In this way, you won't leave your bait-digging patch looking like an open-cast mine. This is important, because when the tide rises an open bait hole can be a real danger to paddling toddlers.

When digging lug it is a good thing to have two plastic buckets – one for undamaged worms, and another for those which have been injured by the fork or spade. Use the damaged ones first.

Alternatively, you can equip yourself with a large partitioned bait-box.

On some lug grounds it is not unusual to come across quantities of white ragworms, and to accommodate these a third partition in the bait-box will come in handy. Never mix lugworm with ragworm.

Storing

Lugworm should never be kept in a metal container. As previously mentioned, they can be collected in a plastic bucket, but my own preference is for a home-made marine-plywood bait-box fitted with removable partitions. The inside of the box should be treated with hot pitch (**NOT** tar) to simplify cleaning, and to prevent the wood absorbing the distinctive, lingering smell of lugworm 'juice'.

Lugworm soon deteriorate in hot weather, and whenever possible they should be stored in a cool, shady

4

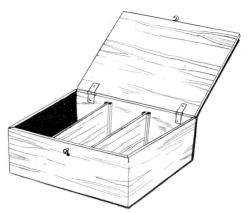

Fig. 3   Bait-box with slotted removable partitions

place. To keep them alive as long as possible, they can be placed between layers of clean newspaper. When doing this, care must be taken not to overcrowd the worms. The best plan is to lay them out in rows about one inch apart, treating them to a change of newspaper when this becomes necessary.

Even under these ideal conditions, however, lugworm are unlikely to remain alive for more than two or three days – and once dead they begin to smell with a power and potency that beggars description.

So be warned – and when carrying a supply of lugworm in your car, make sure that they are safely secured in a leak-proof container. Because, believe me, if only a few escape and die in some inaccessible crevice beneath the floor, you will be doomed to drive for several months with all the windows wide open!

Baiting Up

Lugworm appeal to a wide variety of sea fish, including cod, whiting, plaice, flounders, sole, dabs, wrasse and bass. Naturally, the size of your offering, and the method of presenting it on the hook, will depend on the type of fish you are trying for – and more especially on the size of its mouth and appetite!

When whiting, plaice, flounders, sole or dabs are the quarry it is customary to thread a single medium-sized lugworm on to a fine-wire, round-bend hook. If, before doing this, the worm is first slapped gently against the lid of the bait-box, or some other hard surface, it will immediately stiffen up and become much easier to handle.

There are two ways of threading a lugworm on the hook, and I would suggest you try out both methods and then decide which one you prefer.

First of all there's the 'head-first' method, in which the point of the hook is inserted into the tip of the worm's head. The head section is then eased carefully around the bend of the hook and up the shank. If the worm is long enough it can be taken over the hook-eye and a little way up the nylon snood, leaving an inch or two dangling attractively from the bend of the hook.

The tail of the worm, which is usually full of sand, has little appeal to fish and can be nipped off short if necessary.

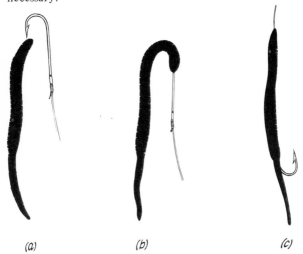

(a)　　　　　　　(b)　　　　　　　(c)

Fig. 4　Three ways of baiting with lugworm.
Method 1.　(a)　Insert hook-point into head;
(b)　Thread body of worm carefully around bend of hook and up the shank. Note the out-jutting tag-end of nylon where the dropper is attached to hook-eye. This helps to hold worm's body in position when casting out.
(c)　The worm ready for casting out. The head has been threaded over the hook-eye and knot, enabling the hook-point to be brought out about a third of the way down the tail.

6

The second method of baiting up requires the hook-point to be inserted where the tail of the worm joins the thicker body. The body of the worm is threaded *backwards* around the bend of the hook, and up the shank, until the hook point is eventually brought out about a quarter of an inch behind the head-end.

Advocates of this latter method declare that soft-bodied lug stay on the hook better when distance casting, and from my own experience I am inclined to agree with this verdict.

If a larger offering is required, consisting of two worms on the one hook, the first worm should be threaded on backwards in the manner just described, followed by a second worm threaded on head-first, with part of it dangling below the bend.

Many anglers use a sliced-shank hook when baiting with lug to prevent the worm from sliding back down the

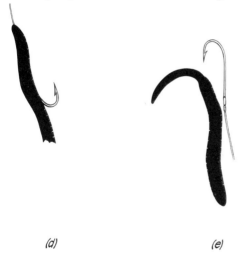

(d)   *(e)*

Method 2. (d) Similar to Method 1, but the hook-point is brought out above the tail and the tail is then nipped off to allow the worm's body juices to emit an attractive scent into the water.
Method 3. (e) Hook-point is inserted where the tail of the worm joins the body. The worm is then threaded backwards on to the hook — the hook-point being brought out just below the head.

shank when casting out. However, sliced-shank hooks tend to be rather thick in the wire, and an alternative method, which can be used with any type of eyed hook, is to leave a projecting stub of nylon when attaching the hook to the dropper snood. This stub of nylon helps to hold the worm firmly in place, in much the same way as the barbs on a sliced-shank hook.

Black Lugworm

The deep-burrowing black lugworm is a much larger and tougher-skinned creature than its more anaemic-looking cousin, the red lug, and it is the angler's favourite when fishing for big cod and bass. Even turbot, brill and rays accept them eagerly when given the opportunity.

Because of its toughness, 'casting off' is rarely a problem when shore fishing with black lug, and the 'head-first' method of baiting up is the one generally used.

When fishing for cod or bass a big black lug is normally used whole on a long-shanked 4/0 or 5/0 hook, but this bait can also be cut into portions and used on smaller hooks for sea bream, plaice, soles, etc.

Black lug are nearly always found at a greater depth than the ordinary red or 'blow' lug, and as a general rule they are also more thinly distributed. Where black and red lug share the same bait ground, the whereabouts of the former can usually be pinpointed by their larger, blackish-hued casts. This is because the deep-burrowing black lug are feeding on a lower stratum of dark, rich muddy sand.

One colony of black lugworm that I have been digging regularly since the mid-1940s is situated in a sheltered West Country estuary where a dense forest of oak trees extends down either side of a steep valley to the water's edge. Leaves falling from the overhanging branches of these waterside trees have, over the centuries, deposited a rich black bed of peaty mud about 18 inches below a top layer of greyish-yellow sand

The top layer of sand contains a population of cockles and reddish-hued blow lug — both useful baits in their own right. But if you dig down another foot or so into the stratum of dark peaty mud, your questing fork will turn up some much larger and firmer-fleshed black lug.

Just after the Second World War, when only a few local weekend anglers used to dig this bait ground, many of these black lug were of truly gigantic proportions. I never actually placed one of them against a tape measure, but at a conservative estimate I'd say the largest ones would easily have exceeded 16 inches in length.

Since those days sea angling has increased tremendously in popularity. As a result, thousands of holiday fishermen visit that part of Cornwall every summer, and the once-deserted bait ground is nowadays dotted with dozens of toiling lug diggers around low tide. They still turn up some black lug, but years of over-digging have reduced their numbers and average size quite dramatically.

As black lugworm go, the ones in this particular West Country estuary are exceptionally easy to dig — and this, of course, is the main reason why they have been over-exploited.

By way of contrast, in some coastal areas black lugworm break all the rules by burrowing almost straight down, instead of lying in the customary U-shaped burrow. This makes them difficult to dig, but their size and usefulness as bait makes the effort well worthwhile.

The customary broad-tined bait fork is not much use when digging for these 'straight-down' lugworm. Instead, you'll need a spade, and the most suitable type is a farmer's draining spade with a long and very narrow blade which tapers to a width of only 2½ inches at the bottom.

Unlike the ordinary shallow-burrowing blow lug, the 'straight-down' black lugworm does not produce a separate tail-cast and blow. Only the tail-cast is in evidence — and this is certainly noticeable enough because, as previously mentioned, its colour is dark and often contrasts with the lighter-hued surface sand.

A closer inspection of the tail-casts will reveal that some have a clear hole through them, and this usually indicates that the worm is fairly close to the surface, instead of being perhaps two feet down.

It usually pays to attack these open burrows first; although it is only fair to add that as soon as you begin digging the worm will start heading downwards. This it can do fairly quickly, because it doesn't have to eat its way into the sand — its burrow is already made.

Digging for these deep-burrowing black lugworm can be hard work, and both speed and care are necessary. This is where the draining spade, with its long and narrow blade, comes in handy. Taking a spot just alongside the tail-cast as a starting point, it enables you to dig quickly downwards along the line of the worm's shaft without having to shift vast quantities of sand.

As the sand is brought to the surface it should be piled in a low wall around the scene of operations to prevent surface water pouring into the hole.

If you watch an expert digging for these lug you will quickly notice how he combines caution with speed. This is because a careless thrust of the spade can easily chop the hidden worm in half.

When you actually catch up with the worm it may be possible to thrust the blade of the spade beneath it in order to prevent any further retreat. However, in an area where the worms grow to a large size, there is a risk that this final thrust of the spade may chop through the lower head section of the worm.

An alternative ruse is to draw the flat of the spade blade backwards across the tail of the worm as soon as it is glimpsed. This turns the tail at right angles to the burrow and halts its downward progress. This gives you time to kneel down and get a grip on it with your fingers.

At this stage it is important to withdraw the worm gently from its burrow without trying to hurry matters. I find that by wiggling my fingers slightly the moist sand around the worm becomes looser, and this helps to break down the suction.

Black lug can be stored between sheets of clean newspaper, in the manner previously described for blow lug. Before use it is customary to nip off the tip of the worm's head, after which the guts are removed by squeezing the body gently between fingers and thumb from tail to head. Rather like squeezing the contents from a tube of toothpaste, in fact!

In this condition the worms stay well on the hook and, unlike the blow lug, they can be dried and deep-frozen, or salted down.

White Ragworm

White ragworm is the name given by sea anglers to pale-coloured marine worms of the genera *Nephtys* and *Glycera*, which are often uncovered when digging for lugworm in clean sand. Other names in common use are 'white cat' (usually applied to *Nephtys*) and 'herringbone' (*Glycera*).

Being rather small (usable white rag are normally about 3 to 5 inches in length) they tend to be ignored by bait-diggers on some parts of the coast. This is a pity because they are a very useful bait – especially when light bottom fishing for dabs, flounders, plaice, sole and gurnard. They also make an exceptionally good offering on float tackle, and when used with this method they will take pollack, mackerel, garfish, bass, mullet, wrasse and – on some parts of the coast – even the occasional sea trout!

These worms are easily recognized by their pearly-white colour, often with a pinkish tinge, and they have a fringe of feet along either side. Unlike the burrow-dwelling lugworm, white ragworm are active predators, and for seizing their prey and burrowing in the sand they are equipped with a remarkably mobile proboscis which is repeatedly extended and retracted when the worm is handled.

Normally white ragworm are found in small colonies in the top layer of sand – often only 6 to 9 inches from the surface. Although they are likely to be present from mid-shoreline downwards in most clean, gently-shelving sandy beaches, both on the open coast and just inside sandy estuaries, the largest worms are often to be found close to where rocks or a stone groyne protrudes upwards through coarse shell-gritty sand.

In such places they are frequently quite numerous, and on occasions when holiday fishing without a bait fork I have dug a day's supply without undue difficulty with my bare hands. This makeshift bait-gathering method has proved particularly useful when shore fishing abroad around the Atlantic shores of Europe.

For example, when holidaying on the Algarve coast of Southern Portugal, I discovered that the local white ragworm, despite their insignificant size, made a first class bait when I was casting off rocks on to adjoining sand for the local 'dourada', or Gilthead Bream. These powerful surf-loving fish put up a tremendous fight on my light bass outfit.

Storing

Although white ragworm and lugworm are often found together on the bait ground, they should never be stored together in the bait-box because liquid oozing from the lugworm will quickly prove fatal to white rag.

Freshly dug white ragworm can be placed in a shallow wooden container between layers of clean, sea-soaked sacking. Kept in this way they'll remain lively for about two days.

Alternatively, you can store the worms in a large glass jar half-filled with sea water. The jar should preferably be fitted with a plastic lid, rather than a metal one. This 'jam jar' method is the one I would recommend if you wish to keep a supply of white ragworm in the domestic refrigerator. Provided you put them in while still absolutely fresh, and remember to change the water every three days, they will remain in good condition for a considerable time.

Baiting Up

When freshly caught, white ragworm are extremely lively little creatures, twisting their rather brittle bodies jerkily to and fro into tight coils. When baiting up, hold them firmly just behind the head. It is essential to use a needle-sharp fine-wire hook for white ragworm, and preferably the hook should also be long-shanked and round in the bend. My own choice is usually a size 2 to 8 Aberdeen, depending on the size of bait and type of fish being sought.

The hook point is inserted just behind the head of the worm, and its body is then threaded carefully around the bend and up the shank to leave some of the tail dangling. When float fishing or driftlining I normally use only one worm, but when bottom fishing in areas where decent-sized bass are expected, it usually pays to thread on another one or two worms below the first one — especially if, as is often the case, the worms are rather small.

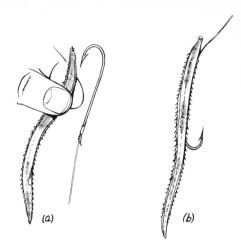

Fig. 5   Baiting up with White Ragworms
(a) Insert hook-point just behind the head;
(b) Thread body of worm around the bend of the hook and
up the full length of the shank to leave the tail dangling.

Cockles

The cockle (*Cerastoderma edule*) is another bait you are likely to come across on your lugworm digging expeditions. These familiar bivalves live near the low tide line on gently shelving shores. They seem to flourish best in areas of clean sand, but also occur quite often where a good deal of mud is mixed with the sand. They are likely to be found in sheltered sandy bays on the open coast, but are equally at home inside estuaries.

Cockles bury themselves about an inch below the surface of the mud or sand, and when covered by the tide they extend their two short tube-like siphons which project slightly above the surface of the sand.

At low tide they retract their siphons and remain hidden to the casual eye, but a slight humping of the sand, and the two tiny blowholes in the sand made by the siphons, will often betray their whereabouts to the experienced bait-hunter.

On most shorelines cockles can be easily unearthed

with a small hand trowel, or even with one's fingers, but the most convenient tool is a garden rake or draw hoe.

Cockles can be opened by inserting the tip of a stubby knife blade between the two halves of the shell and then (preferably with the shell resting on a firm surface) working the blade downwards towards the hinged section.

This enables the two halves to be separated, and the knife blade can then be worked around the inside of the shell to sever the remaining points of attachment and scoop out the bait.

Two or three average-sized cockles, threaded on a fine-wire hook, make an excellent bait for plaice, dabs, whiting, codling and wrasse.

Razorfish

The succulent flesh of the razorfish makes a first-class bait for a wide variety of inshore fish, including bass, plaice, flounders, dabs, gurnards and rays.

Unfortunately razorfish are not always easy to obtain, because these burrowing molluscs are confined to comparatively sheltered areas of firm, gently-shelving sand near the low tide line. Consequently the only worthwhile time to seek this bait on most coasts is during the brief dead low water period around full moon and new moon spring tides.

Razorfish vary slightly in size and coloration from coast to coast, but the species most commonly used as bait (*Ensis siliqua*) is generally about 5 to 7 inches in length. The rather fragile shell is thin, straight and hinged along one side – and it does indeed look very similar to an old-fashioned 'cut-throat' razor with the blade folded into the handle.

From one end of its shell the razorfish protrudes its muscular foot, and from the other end emerge the siphons, or 'breathing tubes'. With the aid of its foot the razorfish burrows almost straight down into the sand. Although capable of descending to a depth of two feet or more, it spends a good deal of its time just below the surface of the sand.

The mouth of a razorfish's burrow is easily recognized by its distinctive keyhole-shaped opening, and it is through this hole that the creature breathes in water and suspended food matter.

Depending on such variable local factors as the tidal range, texture of the sand, and the amount of surface movement of the sand, an experienced bait-gatherer can often judge whether a razorfish is deep down in its burrow, or near the surface. A clearly defined open hole usually shows that its occupant has retreated into the depths; whereas a shallower and less obvious keyhole depression in the sand indicates that the razorfish is just below the surface.

There are several methods of gathering razorfish, but first of all let us take a look at digging. This can, admittedly, be hard work if you attack the burrows indiscriminately, but the job can be made a great deal easier by selecting those 'keyholes' where the surface indications reveal that the razorfish is just below the surface.

The first rule for success is to approach each burrow stealthily. Razorfish are very sensitive to vibrations in the sand, and the careless clumping of gumbooted feet is sufficient to send every self-respecting razorfish for yards around crash-diving to the bottom of its burrow – at the same time sending up an involuntary tell-tale spurt of water.

One old Dorset bait-digger (now retired) used to reduce vibration to a minimum by digging for razorfish in bare feet, both summer and winter. His method was to sink the tines of the bait fork (NOT a spade) just a few inches into the sand. Then, with a quick lift and sideways flick, the upper layer of sand was removed to reveal the razorfish protruding from its burrow.

At this stage one must act very quickly by grabbing the top of the shell and restraining the mollusc from burrowing back down into the sand.

Do not attempt to pull the razorfish out of its burrow by brute force, or you are likely to break the bait. Instead, wait a few seconds, maintaining a steady pressure, until you feel the shellfish loosen its grip. Then you can safely draw it out of the sand.

The advantage of digging razorfish is that the bait is

not damaged in the process, and can be kept alive until required for use.

Spearing razorfish is possibly the easiest method of obtaining this bait once the knack has been acquired. When carried out by a novice, however, a considerable number of baits are likely to be mutilated by the spear — or, worse still, broken and left to rot in the sand. It is hoped that the following hints will enable readers to carry out the job efficiently, and reduce wastage to a minimum.

First of all you will need to make a spear, and this is easily within the capabilities of any amateur handyman. Various types of spear are favoured on different parts of the coast, but an efficient weapon can be made from a mild steel rod about 2½ ft long and ¼-inch diameter.

One end of the rod is heated red-hot and flattened with a hammer until it is about ½-inch wide. This flattened part is then given an arrowhead-shaped point on a grindstone; after which the back edge of the head is trimmed to a barbed shape with a hacksaw. (See diagram). The point should then be heated again, and quenched in water.

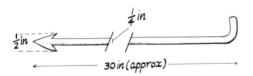

Fig. 6   A home-made razorfish spear

Finally, heat the other end of the rod and bend the last 3 or 4 inches to a right angle to provide a convenient hand-grip.

To use the spear, ease it from a vertical position into the keyhole-shaped entrance to the razorfish's burrow. Do this slowly and gently at first until you feel the shaft of the spear start to slip easily down the burrow.

Some distance down you will feel a very slight resistance as the spear passes through the open shell of the razorfish. Continue thrusting the spear down the burrow for at least another eight or nine inches — or until the spear encounters the bottom of the burrow if

16

the razorfish is down deep. Then, using the right-angled hand-grip as a guide, twist the spear through a quarter circle to set the barbs against the lower end of the razorfish. After that, if all has gone according to plan, your quarry can be drawn out of its hole quite easily.

Salting is a very simple and labour-saving way of gathering razorfish. It possesses the important advantage of ensuring that the bait remains completely unharmed, so that it can be kept alive for a considerable time, or stored in the deep-freezer. All you need is a supply of salt and an empty plastic detergent bottle that has been well rinsed out.

As an economy measure it is best to buy coarse cooking or preserving salt. For convenient handling, and to keep the salt dry on the bait ground, I transfer the loose salt into one of those plastic table salt dispensers which have a small fold-away pouring spout.

Your arrival at the bait ground should be timed to coincide with the final stage of an ebbing spring tide, and the first job will be to fill the plastic detergent bottle with sea water. This can be done quite easily, of course, by wading into the shallows, squeezing the bottle hard to drive out the air, and then dipping it into the sea and releasing the pressure so that water is sucked into the bottle.

Now, armed with a plastic bait bucket, and your plastic bottles of salt and water (some bait hunters also carry a spade, but this is not really essential) you start looking for the distinctive keyhole-shaped breathing holes which mark the entrances to the razorfish burrows.

Approach each selected hole as quietly as possible and pour into it a small quantity of salt. This irritates the razorfish, and if it happens to be lying near the top of its burrow it will rise hurriedly to the surface.

On the other hand, if the mollusc is fairly deep down in its burrow, you will probably have to use a little extra salt and wash it down with a squirt of water from the detergent bottle.

Do not be in too much of a hurry to grab the razorfish as it begins to break the surface, because at the first touch of your probing fingers it will immediately withdraw again into its burrow.

Instead, wait until a couple of inches or so of shell are

17

protruding from the sand, so that you have something substantial to hold on to. Don't try to pull the mollusc forcibly from its hole, because by doing so you will probably break off the foot and spoil its usefulness as a bait.

If you merely hold the shellfish firmly, and prevent it from retreating deeper into its hole, it will quickly relinquish its grip. Then it's simply a matter of lifting it out and popping it into the plastic bucket, which should contain some fresh sea water.

Alternatively, you can save yourself a few seconds' 'grabbing and waiting time' by driving the blade of a spade obliquely beneath the razorfish to cut off its line of retreat.

On a well-stocked razorfish ground a good supply of these molluscs can be gathered during a single low spring tide. However, as the low water period is usually very brief, it pays to tackle the job systematically so that no time is wasted.

Storage
To keep the razorfish alive after you have caught them, it is important to place them in clean water taken from the open sea — NOT from a polluted harbour or muddy estuary. As the numbers of razorfish in the bucket increase, stand them upright — making sure that their breathing siphons are uppermost and there is sufficient water to cover them completely.

Provided that the water is changed at least once daily, and the bucket is stored in a cool, shady place, the razorfish should stay alive for several days. Incidentally, they are likely to spurt water over the side of the bucket, so if you're keeping them indoors it's advisable to cover the bucket with a clean sack and place it on a drip tray.

On the other hand, if you decide to keep your razorfish outdoors, it is advisable to protect them from heavy rain, as this appears to affect them even when they are completely submerged in sea water.

Baiting Up
Razorfish are usually removed from the shell with the aid of a knife, but some anglers prefer to 'pod' them like

18

garden peas, using only finger and thumb pressure. To do this, hold the razorfish horizontally in front of you, with the hinged edges of the shell facing forwards. Then apply pressure with the forefinger and thumb of both hands to the sides of the shell, about an inch or two from the siphon end.

This causes the razorfish to protrude its muscular foot from the opposite end of the shell. Still maintaining pressure on the shell with the left hand, you then grasp the foot with your right hand and ease it gently out through the unhinged side of the shell. A final sharp tug will be needed to sever the ligaments attaching the mollusc to its shell.

It is a simple process once the knack has been acquired, and it leaves the bait in perfect condition for presenting on the hook.

Although a decent-sized razorfish can be cut up to provide two or more portions, I prefer to use this bait whole. It then makes an almost irresistible offering for bass, rays and large plaice.

One popular baiting-up method, specially suitable for shorecasting, is to insert the point of a size 1/0 fine-wire hook about ¾-inch below the siphon end. The bait is then threaded around the bend of the hook, and up the shank, before finally bringing the hook point out through the firm flesh of the foot – leaving an attractive inch or two of the foot dangling free.

Razorfish also make an excellent bait when deep-frozen. There is no need to remove them from the shell before freezing, but they MUST be absolutely fresh.

Clams

Clams are yet another type of bait you are likely to encounter when digging for lugworm in sand or muddy sand. Several species of these burrowing bivalve shellfish are present around our shores, but the two largest and most useful to anglers are *Mya arenaria*, more popularly known as the Gaper Clam, and *Lutraria lutraria*, the Common Otter Shell.

Both make excellent baits when bottom fishing for bass, cod, rays and haddock; whilst a large hook generously baited with two or three bunched clams is almost irresistible to giant common skate.

Mya arenaria which leads a sedentary life beneath beaches of sand and muddy sand, has a distribution range which extends around the English Channel and North Sea coasts, much of Ireland, and the Atlantic beaches of Europe. It is also abundant on many American beaches, where it is highly prized as a sea food.

Clams are usually found in localized colonies, or patches, and their habitat often extends well up the beach. Therefore they can usually be dug over a wide range of tides, including low water neaps. The most likely place to look for them is an area of muddy sand near the mouth of an estuary channel. Although they lie hidden well beneath the surface of the sand or mud, the position of each gaper may be pinpointed by an open round blow hole occupied by the clam's combined inhalant and exhalant siphons, or 'breathing tube'.

A broad-tined bait fork is the best tool for digging the clams out of their burrows. The depth at which they live is limited by the length of their siphons, but as a rough guide an average decent-sized gaper is likely to be about a foot below the surface.

Fig. 7   Surface indication of a clam burrow

Digging for gapers is fairly easy because (unlike razorfish) they are incapable of burrowing any deeper when they sense the disturbance of the digging fork.

When unearthed, the gaper will be revealed as a rather dirty-looking oval-shaped shellfish, with its two hinged valves measuring anything up to six inches long and about three inches broad.

The siphons through which the creature breathes and feeds when buried in the sand have a common protective covering which, being greyish, wrinkled and flexible, resembles a miniature elephant's trunk. However, the traumatic experience of being dug out of its burrow usually makes the clam attempt to retract this siphon tube into its shell — but as this is a physical impossibility the two halves of the shell remain gaping open. Hence the name 'gaper clam'.

Lutraria lutraria is very similar to the gaper in appearance, distribution and habits, but it tends to restrict itself to lower areas of the shoreline. It also favours sandy beaches and mixtures of sand and gravel.

Baiting Up

Both kinds of clam appear to be equally attractive to fish, and to prepare one for baiting up you should first prise open the shell with a thin-bladed knife. When doing this, take care to slant the knife blade so that it scrapes around the rim and inner surface of the shell without slicing through the meaty 'in'ards'.

After cutting off most of the siphon tube, the remainder of the clam meat can be worked on to a fine-wire, round-bend hook, leaving the tough foot of the clam until last so that it rests in the bend of the hook and acts as a support for the softer part of the bait.

Although clam is an excellent bait when used by itself, some shore anglers prefer to use two-hook tackle — one hook being baited entirely with clam in the manner just described, and the other carrying a cocktail

Fig. 8   Lugworm and clam siphon cocktail bait

bait consisting of a lugworm tipped with a 1½-inch section of the clam's siphon tube. When used in this way the siphon should be pulled off (not cut), and then threaded on to the hook tip-first, leaving the frayed meaty end trailing just below the bend.

This not only helps to prevent the lugworm from flicking off the hook when distance casting, but also adds considerably to the appeal of the combined offering, particularly when fishing for bass.

Sandeels

Sandeels are widely distributed around the coasts of Britain and north-west Europe wherever the lower shore-line or sea-bed includes areas of coarse gritty sand. Most sea anglers will already be familiar with these small, slender-bodied fish, because large shoals of them are often to be seen swimming around in the vicinity of harbour walls, or in sandy, rock-encircled coves.

They are an important natural food for many kinds of larger fish, and for this reason they make an excellent bait when shore or boat fishing for bass, pollack, coalfish, cod. rays, turbot, brill, flounders, plaice, gurnard, etc.

Although five species of sandeel are present around our coasts, only two of these — the Lesser Sandeel and the Launce — venture regularly into shallow water. Consequently, these are the ones most commonly used as bait for rod and line fishing. Both have the typical sandeel habit of burrowing into sand when not actively feeding, in order to conceal themselves from predators.

The Lesser Sandeel (*Ammodytes tobianus*) is very abundant close inshore, and is the type most commonly encountered in sandy estuaries and harbours, or buried in sandy beaches near the low water mark during low spring tides. It is a small sandeel, attaining a length of about six or seven inches, and it feeds on various types of zooplankton — tiny marine creatures, none of them larger than a pinhead, that drift to and fro with the tidal currents. The coloration of the Lesser Sandeel is normally sandy-brown on the back and brilliant silver underneath. Its distribution range extends from Portugal northwards as far as Norway and the west Baltic. Around Britain and Ireland it is encountered wherever conditions are suitable, from the lower shoreline to depths of about 15 fathoms.

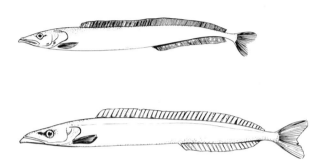

Fig. 9   Lesser sandeel and cock launce

The Cock Launce, or Greater Sandeel, (*Hyperoplus lanceolatus*) is a much larger sandeel. It has been known to attain a length of 18 inches, but the average adult size is more likely to be about ten to twelve inches. It is coloured greenish-blue on the back and silvery underneath, and may be distinguished from *A. tobianus* by the dark mark it carries on its snout just in front of the eyes. Adult launce feed on small free-swimming marine creatures, including young lesser sandeels, and this is the reason why they are often caught by boat anglers when jigging with mackerel feathers, or driftlining with small fish-strip baits. Distribution: Atlantic shores of Europe, English Channel, North Sea and West Baltic, from the inshore shallows to depths of 50 fathoms.

Locating Sandeels
Research by marine biologists has shown that sandeels generally feed during the daytime, and burrow in the sand at night, or during those periods of the day when they are not feeding. In this way they reduce the risk of being eaten by predators – although even so the death

toll is very heavy. It has been calculated that a sandeel's chances of surviving for a year without being gobbled up by a larger fish are only one in four!

Because sandeels spend much of their time hidden from sight beneath the surface of the sand, the bait-hunter must first learn to recognize the type of shore conditions which are most likely to attract these elusive little fish. Points to look for are as follows:

(a) *Coarse, gritty sand*. This type of sand allows the sandeels to burrow into it easily and quickly, and is porous enough to allow oxygen-bearing water to circulate freely beneath its surface. Fine muddy sand, on the other hand, is unsuitable because it tends to 'smother' the sandeels and clogs their gills.

(b) *Fast currents*. Sandeels seem to prefer areas where tides run strongly. This is probably because the scouring currents help to clean the sand in which they lie buried, and at the same time keep it well oxygenated.

Seine Netting for Sandeels

In popular bass fishing resorts, where there is a ready demand for sandeels, two or three local fishermen may combine forces to trap the sandeel shoals on a commercial basis with a small-meshed seine net. Given the right shore conditions — say a small rock-flanked sandy cove that is reasonably free of snags and weed — this is undoubtedly the most efficient method of catching sandeels in large numbers.

A few sea angling clubs that are happily situated in 'sandeel country' keep a sandeel seine for the benefit of their members. The main drawback is the initial cost. To buy a sandeel seine ready made-up at the factory could set you back nearly £200 for a comparatively small net measuring 25 yds long by 6 ft deep. Of course, this figure can be reduced considerably by buying the necessary netting, corks, lines and sinkers, and doing the job yourself.

The fact remains, however, that a seine net is not a practical proposition for the average angler. He needs a much simpler method of catching this bait, and in the following pages I make a number of suggestions which should help to solve this problem.

Fig. 10   Shooting a small fine-meshed seine net to catch sandeel bait

Scraping for Sandeels

Around the shores of Devon and Cornwall, and on many other parts of the coast, dedicated shore anglers have brought sandeel catching to a fine art, using the traditional method of scraping with a launce hook.

An estuary of clean, coarse-grained sand which drains out around low water to form a shallow channel, and maybe a few sandy tide-pools, is the favourite type of shoreline for sandeel hunting. However, gently shelving sandy beaches on the open coast also offer useful possibilities; although, in the latter case, your launce-scraping activities are likely to be restricted to periods around dead low spring tides. A night scraping session during a full-moon spring tide can be particularly productive.

So far as I know, launce hooks are not made commercially, so you cannot simply go into a shop and buy one. Most Cornish anglers make their own from an old

Fig. 11   A launce hook made by grinding down the blade of a stainless steel butcher's knife. A recently caught sandeel is grasped in the bait-hunter's left hand. The glove is a precaution against the venomous spines on the weever fish, which often burrows in the sand in company with the sandeels.

stainless steel butcher's knife, blunting and grinding down the blade to form a hooked end. (See Fig. 11.)

To do its job efficiently, the blade must be sufficiently long (about 8½ to 10 inches) to probe well down into the sand. It must also be thin enough to offer little resistance when slicing through the sand; although, at the same time, it must not be *too* thin, otherwise it will become too flexible and springy in use.

Experts in the art of launce scraping (and believe me it *is* an art) usually wade about calf-deep in the shallows, working their hooked blade in the submerged sand in a systematic figure-of-eight movement.

After each patch of sand has been explored with the blade, the launce hunter advances a yard or two and then repeats the process. When working an estuary channel he usually advances against the current.

When the searching blade contacts a sandeel a slight

26

resistance is felt, and an upwards movement of the blade combined with a downwards movement of the free hand traps the sandeel in the hooked end of the blade. This requires a fair degree of skill, and the beginner would probably be well advised to choose a low spring tide for his first attempt. This will enable him to practise in the damp sand at the water's edge, so that he can actually see the sandeel as it is brought to the surface.

Then, as he acquires the knack, he can enter the shallows and try his luck in just a few inches of water.

Incidentally, sandeels are not the only creatures which live beneath the sand in this sort of habitat. Venomous-spined weever fish are also quite numerous and may be hooked up by the blade of the launce scraper. Therefore, in order to avoid injury and considerable pain, it is essential to wear a thick industrial type

Fig. 12   Two anglers scraping for sandeels in a Cornish estuary, using the launce hook and plastic glove method.

plastic glove on the catching hand. One useful dodge which I learned from Stan Hosking, a well-known Cornish shore angler and bait-hunter, is to cut out a tiny hole in each finger-tip of the glove to make it 'self-draining'.

A freshly-caught sandeel, wriggling frantically in its efforts to escape, is a very slippery customer to handle. So it's essential to have something to pop your captive into as soon as it is lifted from the water, and the best plan is to equip yourself with a linen catch-bag fitted with a couple of strong tapes. This is tied in front of your midriff, like a kangaroo's pouch. Of course, it soon becomes soaked with water, but this helps to keep the sandeels alive.

At the end of the bait-catching session the sandeels can be transferred into a small cool-box, along with a few lumps of ice, if you intend to use them the same day. In this way they can be transported to a distant

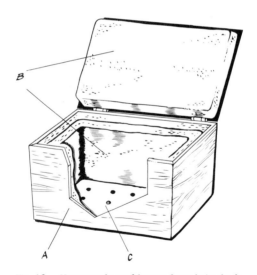

Fig. 13   Home-made cool-box to keep baits fresh
A – Outer casing made of marine grade plywood: B – Expanded
polystyrene insulating material covered with aluminium foil;
C – Removable plastic inner base. This stands on small lugs
to raise it about ½-inch above the bottom of the cool box. It
is drilled with about a dozen holes to allow water from
melting ice cubes to drain away from the bait.

shore fishing spot, and even on a hot summer's day they will be still alive several hours later.

So far as surfcasting is concerned, it doesn't really matter a great deal if the sandeels are dead, provided they remain fresh and firm-fleshed — and they will remain in this condition for at least two days if stored in a cool-box.

Most shop-bought cool-boxes are unnecessarily large and cumbersome for bait-storage purposes, but it is a simple job to make a small cool-box at home out of scrap materials. I made mine from a few offcuts of marine plywood (a common beachcombing find), and insulated it with some thin slabs of expanded polystyrene ('plastic foam') packing material. The inside of the box is then lined with aluminium foil, which is stuck to the plastic foam with a waterproof adhesive.

Digging for Sandeels

On certain localized areas of sandy shoreline it is often possible to uncover useful quantities of sandeels by simply flicking over the sand near the low tide mark to a depth of a few inches, using quick scooping movements with the tines of a bait-digging fork.

Mind you, it's no good using this bait-hunting method in just any old patch of damp sand. As mentioned previously, sandeels prefer to conceal themselves in coarse shell-grit or pulverised shale. Sandeels also favour areas which are scoured by fast currents, and for this reason they are often found in the vicinity of estuary-mouth 'bottlenecks', or in the sandbanks which tend to build up just outside or inside the mouth of an estuary.

As the sandeels are flicked to the surface by the tines of the fork they must be grabbed very quickly, because if given half a chance they'll vanish into the damp sand again as if by magic. Not for nothing are they known as 'quicksilver bait' on some parts of the coast.

Ideally, therefore, sandeel gathering is a job for two people — one to use the bait fork, and the other to pounce upon the sandeels as soon as they are flicked out of the sand.

When you hit a good patch of shoreline, and the

sandeels are being turned up thick and fast, the task of catching them becomes both energetic and exciting. If you take on the hob of 'grabber', you must be careful not to let your haste and excitement overcome your sense of caution.

If you grab recklessly at a weever fish, believing it to be a sandeel, it is likely to be a week or two before you hold a rod again. The best safeguard against this danger is to wear a protective glove, as recommended in the previous section.

It is also fatally easy for a hurriedly outstretched hand to get in the way of the bait fork that is being wielded energetically by your partner.

There is even a risk of self-inflicted injury. For example, during a sandeel-catching foray in an estuary on the south coast of Ireland, I was once careless enough to drive a fork tine right through one of my waders. By little short of a miracle the needle-sharp prong passed between two of my toes without drawing blood.

A local fisherman, who happened to be sandeel-catching nearby, overheard me cursing the puncture in my wader. 'Sure,' he told me, with some justification, 'It isn't angry you should be, but offering up thanks for a lucky escape.'

To prove his point, he told me the sad tale of a local farmer who went wading in the estuary one moonlit night in the hope of spearing a few flatfish with a dung fork. In the near-dark this farmer drove the fork through his own foot, and within a fortnight he had died of blood-poisoning.

So you see it pays to be careful — even in this age of antibiotics.

The 'Splash and Commotion' Method

Some friends and I discovered this method of catching sandeels by chance several years ago while on a bass fishing holiday at Rosscarbery — a pleasant little Irish coastal resort situated at the head of a sandy estuary. At low tide this estuary dries out almost completely, except for a few shallow pools and channels which meander among the extensive lug-castled sandflats.

For the first few days of our holiday these lug beds were the main source of bait when fishing the

*Fig. 14   Catching sandeels by the 'splash and commotion'
method*

magnificent local surf beaches. However, during our
daily lug-digging expeditions we noticed that the estuary
channels were also swarming with sandeels. With little
explosive puffs of sand they spurted out of the shallows
in front of our feet as we waded across the tide-pools. It
was easy to see why the local bass foraged up these
channels as soon as the tide began to flood!

We badly wanted to catch some of these sandeels for
bait. It would have been easy to do this with the help of
a launce hook or small-meshed rake-net, but lacking
either of these items we had to seek an alternative
method.

We eventually decided that our best plan would be to
flush the sandeels out of the sand by wading down the
channel in line abreast, and then drive them ashore on
the banks of the channel. There we would be able to
grab them; or alternatively, if they disappeared quickly
into the sand, we could dig them out again with our bait
forks.

There were five of us, and between us we had three
digging forks. I took up position in the middle of a
narrow bottleneck in the channel, and the others formed
themselves into a line facing me, about 40 yards higher

up the channel. With a terrific splashing of waders and bait forks they began to drive the sandeels before them, and as the tiny silver-glinting creatures came streaking towards me I also began stamping and swirling my bait fork to and fro in the water. My job was to act as a human 'cork' in the bottleneck.

Suddenly, as the line of beaters drew closer, the sandeels began to leave the water. In ones and two at first; then in their dozens, they appeared wriggling and burrowing on the banks of the channel. The two 'wing' men, who were unencumbered with forks, dived on them and began popping them into plastic bags.

But our biggest haul was to come a minute or two later, after we had stopped churning up the water. As the water began to clear we were surprised to see many more sandeels lying motionless on the sandy bed of the channel.

At first glance they appeared to be dead, but in fact they were quite unharmed and were soon wriggling around in the bait box as vigorously as the first ones we had captured.

At the time we decided that the unconscious sandeels must have been in a state of shock. However, I have used this method of catching sandeels on many occasions since then, and have noticed a rather curious thing. When the water is churned up by beaters armed with forks we usually gather up large numbers of unconscious sandeels; whereas when sticks, spades or oars are used instead of forks, comparatively few sandeels are picked up unconscious — although plenty leave the water and are picked up on the banks.

The reason for this, I believe, is that the tines of a fork vibrate when swirled vigorously through the water. In fact, if the tines of the fork happen to be worn and thin they actually emit a high-pitched whining noise. It seems reasonable to assume, therefore, that the sandeels are affected in some way by these underwater sound waves.

Needless to say, the above method of catching sandeels is only practicable in estuaries where the low-tide channels are shallow and narrow. Also, of course, you'll need at least four or five 'beaters' to be sure of worthwhile results.

Fig. 15   A sandeel rake-net

Rake-Netting for Sandeels

In shallow tide-pools, both inside sandy estuaries and on open beaches, good catches of sandeels can often be made with the help of a home-made rake-net (see Fig. 15).

The piece of wood for the cross-beam of the rake measures 24 in x 5 in x 2 in — or, if you prefer, you can use two one-inch-thick pieces of timber. Suitable driftwood for the job can be picked up on most beaches, but be sure it is close-grained and free of knots.

Cut the timber to a wedge shape (Fig. 16(a)), and plane it smooth. The 'teeth' of the rake are half-a-dozen six-inch nails, driven through the block at an angle so that they slant forwards. To avoid splitting the wood,

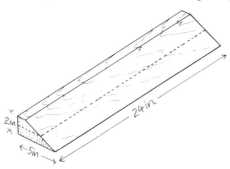

Fig. 16 (a). First make the wedge-shaped cross-beam, with dimensions as shown. The dotted line indicates position of join if the cross-beam is cut from two 1-inch-thick pieces of timber.

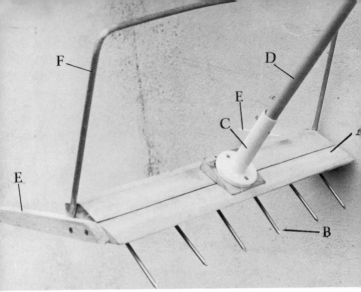

*Fig. 16 (b).   The components of the rake-net. A – cross-beam;
B – 6-inch nails; C – handle socket (made from old lamp holder);
D – broom handle; E – hardwood net supports, approximately
11 inches long; F – net frame made from old TV aerial antenna.
(Frame folds flat for easy stowage.)*

holes should be drilled to provide a tight driving fit for
the nails, and each hole should be countersunk to
accommodate the nail-heads.

If you have made the wedge-shaped block from two
one-inch-thick pieces of timber, you can fit the nails
through the lower half of the block before screwing on
the top half. This adds about another inch to the length
of the teeth, which in my experience is a considerable
advantage on many coasts.

Next the block is fitted with a broom handle, and it is
worth taking care to fit this at the right angle to suit
your height. The handle can be socketed directly into
the centre of the cross-beam, but in the rake-net
pictured here I have made the handle easily detachable
for stowing in the boot of a car.

This can be achieved in various ways, but I made use
of an old brass electric wall light bracket that was lying
about in my workshop. After hacksawing off the end
carrying the bulb socket, I was left with a flanged tube
that just fitted the handle.

34

A hole was then drilled through the tube and handle to take a galvanized retaining pin. To prevent the pin from getting lost accidentally, it was fitted with a lanyard.

The hooped framework for the netting can be made out of any convenient materials you happen to have by you. In the past I have used pliable wands cut from a withy bush, and − more recently − the aluminium antenna from a discarded TV aerial.

It is a good idea to make the hoop fold flat for easy stowage. This can be done quite simply by flattening and drilling each end of the tubing to take a 1¼-inch brass screw. One screw is fitted into each end of the cross-beam, thus leaving the hooped rod free to swivel. When the net is in use the hoop is raised and tied to the handle.

Sandeels are elusive little creatures, so the netting must have a very fine mesh. I use prawn netting (10mm mesh) for the jaws of the net, tapering to lant netting (5mm mesh) towards the bunt.

Nylon netting is best because it dries quickly, and this makes it lighter to carry and more convenient to transport in a car. To prevent the wooden framework from absorbing water it is advisable to paint it, preferably in a sandy-brown colour.

To use the rake-net, first choose a spot where sandeels are likely to be hiding − then wade slowly and quietly into the inshore shallows. Extend the net seawards, then draw it towards you with a raking movement. If sandeels are present they will be flushed out by the approaching teeth, and will instinctively head towards deeper water − and into the net!

Storing Sandeels

Having gone to considerable trouble to obtain your supply of fresh sandeels, you will naturally wish to keep them for as long as possible in top condition, so that they retain their maximum appeal for fish.

If you are an inshore dinghy angler the solution is likely to be a fairly simple one. After the sandeels have been caught they are transferred as quickly as possible to a perforated wooden courge, which is then towed behind the boat on the journey out to the fishing mark. The

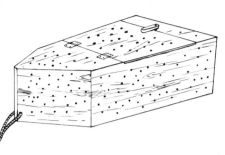

Fig. 17   *Livebait courge. A courge, for storing sandeels, peeler crabs and similar livebaits, can be made from marine plywood. Its forward end is pointed, for ease of towing behind a boat, and the holes must be numerous and small. It is a good idea to finish off the holes with a red hot metal skewer, in order to remove any rough splinters of wood on the inside of the holes.*

constant stream of water flowing through the dozens of tiny holes in the courge helps to keep the sandeels lively.

Throughout the fishing session the courge remains floating alongside the boat – a small flap-up lid enabling anglers in the boat to extract a sandeel whenever a fresh bait is required.

Unfortunately a courge will not solve the shore angler's sandeel storage problems. Very often he has to transport his bait for long distances in the boot of a car, and on arrival at the fishing venue the bait container is likely to remain for many hours on a sunny beach or rock.

One makeshift storage method is to place the sandeels in a plastic box or bucket between layers of clean, sea-soaked hessian sacking. Treated in this way they will remain alive for several hours, but before the day is over they are likely to become limp and lifeless.

A far better method is to store the sandeels in the small home-made marine-plywood cool-box described earlier in this chapter. If the cool-box is partly filled with a few lumps of ice, the sandeels will remain fresh and firm-fleshed throughout a whole day's fishing.

However, the angler who lives fairly close to a sandeel-catching estuary or strand can do even better than this. By equipping himself with a fish tank and aerator he can keep a supply of live sandeels always ready for use at home, so that bait need never be a problem whatever the state of the tide or weather.

When several anglers are in the habit of fishing together, and sharing the task of bait-gathering, they could hardly do better than adopt the system used by Stan Hosking and Mike Osborne, of Camborne, in Cornwall. In Stan's garage there is a large plastic tank about two-thirds full of sea water, and this is kept constantly aerated by an aquarium-type air pump driven off the electric mains.

Sandeels taken by scraping or seine-netting in the nearby Hayle estuary are quickly transferred to this tank, and if necessary they could be kept alive for several weeks. In actual fact, however, Stan and Mike (and their numerous pals) put in so many shore fishing hours between them that few of the sandeels spend more than two or three days in the tank before they are scooped out again for use as bait.

The success of these North Cornwall shore anglers is pretty awe-inspiring. Bass, tope, rays and pollack are all taken with enviable consistency from their favourite shore and rock hotspots. Needless to say, skill and local knowledge play a major part in their success, but I think they would be the first to agree that another important contributory factor is their constant supply of livebait.

Of course, the average weekend fisherman is more likely to be seeking a simple way of keeping a couple of dozen sandeels alive overnight, so that after being caught during a Saturday low tide they will still be in tip-top condition for a spell of float fishing off the rocks on Sunday.

One way to achieve this is to fit a small battery-powered aerator to the side of a plastic bucket half-filled with sea water. Figure 18 shows an inexpensive and very efficient portable livebait container made from one of those plastic tubs with a clip-on lid in which decorating products are sometimes sold.

By inserting the plastic air pipe through the top of the container, the aerator can do its job while the lid is clipped in place. In the centre of the lid a circular hole is cut, and then covered with a slightly larger disc of stiff plastic which swivels on a single small brass nut and bolt. The object of this, of course, is to allow sandeels to be

Fig. 18   A home-made livebait container equipped with a battery-powered aerator. Beside it lies a launce hook.

taken out of the container as and when required, without repeatedly removing the lid.

The swivelled plastic flap fits tightly enough to prevent water slopping out of the container while it is being carried around. At the same time, however, it isn't airtight, so air from the rising bubbles is able to escape quite freely.

Deep-Freezing Sandeels

Sandeels can be stored successfully in the domestic freezer. They are best placed, about a dozen at a time, in small plastic bags from which all air has been squeezed out, and then sealed carefully. When required for use, they should be left in the bag until fully thawed out. Do not make the common mistake of trying to thread them on the hook while they are still half-frozen.

Frozen sandeels are not recommended for trolling, float fishing or spinning, but they make a perfectly good bottom fishing bait in situations where long-distance casting is not required. They will be accepted eagerly by thornback and small-eyed rays, and also by bass provided that no other angler fishing nearby is using fresh or live sandeel!

Baiting Up with Sandeels

Sandeels can be used as bait for a wide variety of fishing methods, including bottom fishing (shore and boat), float fishing, driftlining, trolling, spinning and surf-casting. The species of fish taken by these methods include bass, pollack, coalfish, mackerel, garfish, scad, shad, sea trout, turbot, brill, rays, whiting, cod, flounders, plaice (particularly in West Country waters) and gurnard.

The methods of baiting up also vary widely to suit the fishing method being used, and (to a lesser degree) the type of sea conditions encountered locally.

Figures 19(a) to (e) show some of the more popular methods of baiting up:

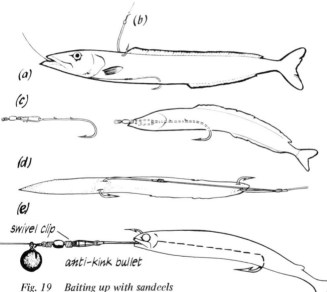

Fig. 19   Baiting up with sandeels
(a) Baiting with live sandeel when driftlining or slow trolling;
(b) Baiting with live sandeel when float fishing;
(c) Method of baiting with a dead fresh sandeel when bottom fishing, including surfcasting. When distance casting, the mouth of the sandeel is tied over the lower swivel eye with light nylon line. This bait is normally presented on a single-hook leger trace or running paternoster.
(d) Baiting with a fillet cut from the side of a greater sandeel (a popular offering when legering for turbot or brill);
(e) Spinning with dead sandeel on tandem hook tackle.

Slipper Limpets

The Slipper Limpet (*Crepidula fornicata*) is a comparatively recent newcomer to British and European waters.

During the latter half of the last century some young seed oysters were imported from America to restock Britain's depleted oyster beds. These American oysters did not breed in their new environment because water temperatures around our shores were too low to suit their spawning requirements. However, some slipper limpets which had been accidentally introduced with the seed oysters found our local sea conditions very much to their liking, and their numbers increased with astonishing rapidity.

The presence of these slipper limpets off the south-east coast was first noted in the 1880s, and less than a hundred years later, at the time of writing this book, they have spread right around the south and south-west coasts as far as Wales, and northwards up the east coast as far as Scotland. More recently they have also spread to parts of the Dutch, Danish and German coasts — possibly after a few had 'hitched a lift' across the North Sea attached to a ship's anchor or a trawler's fishing gear.

The popularity of slipper limpet as a sea angling bait is spreading almost as fast as the colonising progress of the shellfish itself, and every year sees many more anglers making use of it. A wide variety of fish can be caught on it, but it is particularly useful when fishing for bass, flounders, sea bream (both black and red) and wrasse.

Because slipper limpets normally live in shallow water, beyond the limits of the lowest tides, they cannot be obtained by any of the usual bait collecting methods. However, during onshore gales they are often washed up along suitable stretches of gently shelving shoreline, and the angler who does a bit of beachcombing after a spell of stormy weather can often find scores of these shellfish stranded along the high water line.

Slipper limpets are gregarious creatures, and are usually found in clusters of four, five, six or even more — each shellfish except the lowermost one being

Fig. 20   A 'chain' of slipper limpets

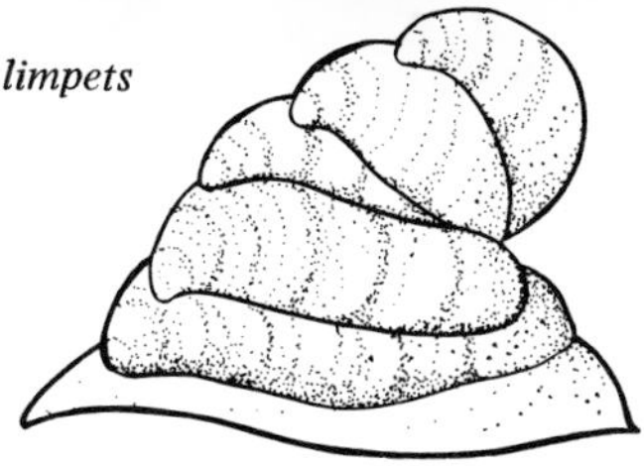

attached firmly to the back of its neighbour. An interesting thing about these 'chains' of slipper limpets is the fact that the oldest shellfish in the group is always the one at the bottom of the chain, and they become progressively younger towards the top. Another rather unusual thing is that the topmost shellfish are males, but as they grow older and work their way down the chain they change into females.

Slipper limpets will also attach themselves individually to sea-bed stones or oyster shells, and these 'loners' become females without passing through the preliminary male stage. Indeed, when present on oyster beds they become a serious pest, literally smothering the oysters to death. Contrary to popular belief, they do not prey on the oysters. In fact they feed like the oysters themselves on planktonic matter suspended in the water.

Storing

Slipper limpets washed up on the shore will keep best if gathered early in the morning before they become dried out by sun and wind. They should be placed in a clean, sea-soaked hessian sack, and preferably kept in a shady outbuilding with a cool stone floor. Stored in this way they will remain alive for a week or more. Alternatively, they can be kept alive for considerably longer if placed in the type of aerated keep-tank described in the chapter on Sandeels.

Should you ever find yourself with more slipper limpets than you can conveniently store alive, the surplus can be shelled and either salted down or deep-frozen.

Baiting Up

To prepare slipper limpets for baiting up, you must prise apart each individual shellfish in the chain and then

41

extract the occupant from its shell. This is best done with a mussel skeining knife, which can be easily made by grinding down the blade of an old table knife.

First of all, loosen the foot of the limpet by running the rounded tip of the knife between the foot and all surfaces adjoining the opening in the shell – including the shelf-like projection inside the shell.

Then, lifting the foot with the knife blade, grip it between your fingers and pull it gently towards the rounded end of the shell – whereupon the 'in'ards' should slide out from beneath the shelf without difficulty.

It is best to prepare a good quantity of slipper limpets in this way at the start of a fishing session, as this avoids delay in baiting up and makes for more productive fishing.

Whenever possible use a fine-wire hook for slipper limpet, and begin by working the point and shank through the softer parts of the shellfish, leaving the muscular foot until last to provide support for the remainder of the bait.

When fishing for flounders or wrasse I usually mount two or three slipper limpets on a size 1/0 hook, but larger fish, such as bass and cod, are best coaxed with a more generous offering of six on a long-shanked 5/0.

Part Two
Baits from Rocky and Mixed Shorelines

Peeler and Soft Crabs

Big bass are blessed with more than their fair share of native cunning, and in calm estuary waters they'll often ignore a legered lugworm or king ragworm. But there's one bait that even the most wily old bass has difficulty in refusing – and that's a peeler crab.

For the benefit of readers who are new to sea angling, perhaps I had better begin by explaining just what is meant by a 'peeler' crab.

Like all other crustacea, the familiar greenish-brown shore crab (*Carcinus maenus*) can only grow bigger by occasionally shedding its hard shell. A peeler crab, therefore, is simply one that is preparing to cast off its old suit of armour, and the angler wishing to use it as bait merely hastens the 'peeling' process by stripping off the old shell to expose the new soft shell underneath.

In this condition the crab is easy to mount on the hook, and makes a very attractive bait that is relished not only by bass but also by flounders, cod, pollack, thornback rays and many other kinds of sea fish.

A crab which has just completed its moulting process is known as a 'softback'; but after a day or two the new shell begins to harden, and it then becomes a 'paperback' or 'leatherback', and finally a 'hardback'. As this new shell hardens up, the crab becomes less and less useful for hook bait.

Season and Habitat

Peeler and soft crabs are usually most plentiful around June, but on suitable types of shoreline they can be found in reasonable numbers right through the summer and well into autumn. Needless to say, problems are likely to arise during the peak holiday months, when the increased demand outstrips the available supply. It is then necessary to arrive on the shore early during the low tide periods if you wish to beat other bait-hunters to the most productive crabbing spots.

The most likely places to look for peelers are sheltered estuaries, creeks or enclosed bays where the shoreline is composed of wrack-draped rocks bordered by soft mud or muddy sand. However, they may also be plentiful on the open coast where conditions are suitable. In fact, wherever there are hardbacked shore crabs and small edible crabs there are also bound to be peeler and soft crabs of the same species.

The discarded kettles and old saucepans which inevitably accumulate on the muddy bottom of a tidal harbour are also likely to yield peeler crabs. So, too, are the nooks and crannies near the weedy base of a sea-eroded harbour wall or breakwater.

Instinct tells a peeler crab that it is going to become very vulnerable and attractive to all sorts of predators

Fig. 21   Gathering peeler crabs at low tide. On this type of shoreline, consisting of mixed rock and sand, the crabs are likely to be found hiding beneath the trailing clumps of bladderwrack. Quite often, to obtain additional concealment, the peeler crabs will also partly bury themselves in the soft sand or mud.

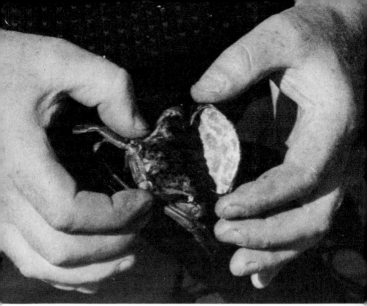

Fig. 22 A peeler crab with its old shell partly removed, revealing the soft new shell forming underneath

during the moulting process, so it conceals itself in a rock crevice, or partly buries itself in the mud behind a curtain of bladderwrack.

With a little practice the bait-hunter soon learns to recognize these likely hiding places, and he also develops an 'eye' for piercing the shore crab's natural camouflage.

It is unwise to search for these buried crabs with your bare fingers owing to the risk of injury on sharp-edged fragments of shell, broken glass and other hazards. Instead, it is much wiser and easier to do your scratching and probing with a short length of ¼-inch mild steel rod, bent at one end into the shape of a hook. This useful implement can also be used to reach into likely crevices beneath the larger rocks.

Besides unearthing peeler and soft crabs from these crevices, the crab hook sometimes drags out a welcome bonus in the shape of a lobster or edible crab.

The main problem confronting the novice bait-hunter lies in distinguishing the all-too-few peelers from the hundreds of useless and rapidly scuttling hardbacks. (Actually hardbacks *can* be useful when wrasse fishing, as we shall see later on in this chapter).

Fairly early in your search you will probably come upon a pugnacious male crab clasping a second crab to his abdomen. The male will be a hardback, but you may be sure that the other crab is a female peeler or softback.

Another clue to look out for is coloration. The shell of a peeler usually has a dull, somewhat chalky appearance, and on being disturbed it lacks the aggressive attitude of a normal hardback. Nor does it scuttle away so quickly, and quite often will remain cowering in its hiding place.

When in doubt the matter can be put to the test by pressing your thumb-nail against the side of the carapace — whereupon there should be a slight movement or separation where it overlaps the lower half of the shell.

If still in doubt, the final positive test is to break off one of the crab's legs close to a joint. If the shell comes away with bits of tendon attached to it you may be sure the crab is a hardback. On the other hand, if the shell slides off the crab's leg cleanly, like a wellington boot being removed from a foot, then the crab is a peeler.

Incidentally, this test does not bother the crab unduly, and at the next moult it will grow a new leg. It is not a thing I like to do more than necessary, but at least it prevents hardbacked crabs from being killed unnecessarily through faulty identification.

Peeler crabs can be kept alive for several days if stored in a wooden or plastic container under some freshly gathered damp seaweed, preferably in a cool and shady outhouse. Alternatively, they can be kept in a floating livebait courge, tied to a boat mooring.

Softbacks, which must be kept apart from peelers, should be used as quickly as possible; otherwise they will turn into hardbacks again!

Baiting Up

For humane reasons I prefer to kill each crab before placing it on the hook. This is done by lifting the flap-like 'apron' beneath the crab's abdomen, and then stabbing the exposed part with a thin-bladed knife or baiting needle.

Before baiting up with a peeler crab, the carapace is lifted off by inserting a thumb-nail under the back edge.

46

As previously mentioned, this exposes the new soft shell underneath.

After that the two claws are removed whole, and then the undershell is peeled away, beginning with the mouth end and working back towards the tail-flap or apron.

A smallish peeler crab is best used whole, but large ones can be cut in half.

Fig. 23   Baiting up with a peeler crab

Different anglers have their own favourite methods of mounting a whole peeler crab. The method I have been using with success for many years is to break off one leg at the point where it is attached to the crab's body. The hook-point is then inserted into the exposed leg socket, and brought out through the crab's fleshy back. Having done this, the crab is fixed firmly to the hook with a few turns of elasticated crimping thread, obtainable from any draper's shop. The thread is first wound tightly around the hook shank three or four times (no knots are required); then around the crab's body several times so that each loop passes between two pairs of legs. Finally the other end of the thread is fastened off around the hook shank again with a series of half-hitches.

Some anglers prefer to wind several turns of elasticated thread around the peeler crab BEFORE mounting it on the hook. Here again the thread should be wound in criss-cross fashion between the legs so that there is no risk of the turns working loose when casting. The hook, which should match the size of the crab, can then be inserted through the tail-flap of the crab, brought out through the back, and then (with a 180 degree twist) thrust through the crab's body again so that the hook-point finally emerges through the abdomen.

Whichever method you decide to use (and both are good) it is essential to use a hook with a sufficiently large gape, so that the hook point stands slightly proud

47

of the bait and can be driven into the fish efficiently when striking at a bite. My own preference is for a round-bend hook, such as the 'Model Perfect'.

Large peeler crabs after being 'de-shelled', are best divided down the middle with a sharp knife in a 'fore and aft' direction, so that each half includes part of the head end and part of the tail end. The two claws are broken off first for use as separate baits.

Each half-portion of body should first be wrapped with several turns of elasticated thread, before mounting it on the hook. Again it is best to use a round-bend hook, and to insert the point first of all through the tail-end and then back through the body again so that the bait is held securely in the bend of the hook.

The claws, with their shells removed, can be threaded whole on a fine-wire round-bend hook. Depending on the size of fish being sought, and the supply of bait available, they can either be presented singly, or mounted one above the other on a long-shanked hook.

Hardbacked Crabs

As most experienced sea anglers will already know, hardbacked shore and swimming crabs feature prominently in the diet of many saltwater fish. Proof of this is often forthcoming when one is gutting a decent-sized bass or cod, for it is not at all unusual to find the fish's stomach filled with the chomped-up remains of these shellfish.

For some mysterious reason, however, hardbacked crabs seem to lose their attraction to fish as soon as they are used as hook bait. The one notable exception to this rule is the ballan wrasse.

Around rocky stretches of shoreline in the West Country and the Channel Islands these sporting and colourful fish attain a very good size, and these big wrasse like nothing better than a hook offering of crab. With their powerful crushing teeth they are able to make short work of a small to medium-sized hardbacked crab, which they will attack just as eagerly as a peeler or softback crab.

The method of baiting up with hardbacks depends partly on the fishing technique being used, and partly on the size of the crab. If you are bottom fishing off a rock ledge, and only need to lob the bait a few yards into fairly calm water, it may be sufficient to insert the hook-point through the top of the shell between the eyes, and then snick the point of the hook through the tail end of the crab.

An alternative method entails threading the crab on to a treble hook and 15lb b.s. nylon trace with the aid of a baiting needle. First kill the crab by lifting the abdominal flap, or 'apron', and piercing the centre of the exposed area with the baiting needle.

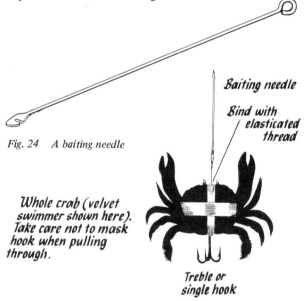

Fig. 24   A baiting needle

Baiting needle

Bind with elasticated thread

Whole crab (velvet swimmer shown here). Take care not to mask hook when pulling through.

Treble or single hook

Fig. 25   Method of baiting up with hardbacked crab, using a treble hook and a baiting needle

Then thread the nylon trace attached to the treble hook lengthways through the crab, using the baiting needle to draw the trace in at the tail-end and out between the eyes. (See Fig. 25.) In rough sea conditions

49

a few turns of elasticated thread around the crab will help to make the bait more secure.

One final word of warning. Never bait up with a live hardbacked crab. Quite apart from the humane considerations, a live crab will either tangle up your terminal tackle, or will snag it up by crawling under the nearest rock.

Prawns

Several species of prawn suitable for use as bait inhabit the shallow waters around our shores, and the largest of these is the Common Prawn (*Leander serratus*) which attains a length of about four inches, excluding the antennae. Its distribution range extends from the Mediterranean northwards around the Atlantic coastline of Europe, including Britain and Ireland, and into the English Channel.

To avoid any possible confusion, it should perhaps be explained that the so-called Dublin Bay Prawn, or 'Scampi' Prawn (*Nephrops norvegicus*), although considerably larger, is in fact more closely related to our lobsters and crayfish. It lives in fairly deep water, and is never found on the shore.

The true prawns used as sea angling baits, on the other hand, abound in weed-draped rocky tide-pools during the summer months, and they are also plentiful close inshore just beyond the low tide line. In the autumn the rock pool prawns begin to move down the shore into sub-littoral waters, where they remain throughout the winter.

Two other members of the prawn tribe (*Leander squilla* and *L. adspersus*) are very similar in general appearance to *serratus* and are found in the same kind of shore conditions. Their average size, however, is smaller and their distribution range slightly wider, extending from the Mediterranean to the North Sea and parts of the Baltic.

A live prawn, presented on light float or driftline tackle, makes a first-class bait for pollack or bass, and similar offerings (either dead or alive) are also relished by wrasse, pouting, gurnard and many other kinds of fish. More detailed information on baiting up with prawn will be found later in this chapter.

Hand Netting

On some types of coastline prawns become trapped at low tide in small longshore rock pools, and it is possible to scoop them out quite easily with a child's dip-net. The only snag is that prawns found under these conditions are usually rather small.

Prawns of a much better size can often be netted during low spring tides in sheltered rock gullies opening out into deeper water, and also in the larger type of rock pool or lagoon that is formed by numerous weed-draped boulders. For best results, the boulders should be bedded on a bottom of mud or muddy-sand.

For prawning on this type of shoreline you will need a good quality hand-net with a metal pear-shaped frame. In the West Country we favour a strong galvanized frame that is tilted up at a slight angle to the handle, and to prevent the netting from becoming frayed against rocks, the meshes are attached to the lower side of the frame by means of a lacing of copper wire passing through small copper split-pins.

The prawns are likely to be hiding in rock crevices and amongst the festoons of weed, so the net should be worked into these places with a quick upwards and backwards scooping movement. When working the net through thick weed, the scooping action should be combined with some vigorous shaking movements in order to dislodge any prawns which may be clinging to the weed.

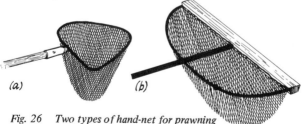

Fig. 26   Two types of hand-net for prawning
(a) pear-shaped net with galvanized iron frame;
(b) wooden-boomed push-net for use where rocks are
surrounded by soft sand or mud.

Fig. 27   Push-netting for prawns around the sandy fringes of a rocky outcrop

Hand-netting for large prawns nearly always entails wading, often up to the waist. On a warm summer's day, wearing swimming trunks and canvas shoes, this is a pleasant enough occupation. But in chilly weather a pair of chest waders will be appreciated.

Waders with hobbed soles are preferable because these reduce the risk of slipping on the treacherous green silk weed. A haversack for the catch completes the outfit, and this should be fitted with a flap to prevent the catch escaping when wading deep.

Another type of hand-net, fitted with a broad wooden boom, is used on certain parts of the coast — particularly in tidal estuaries and creeks where a bottom of soft muddy sand runs in close around small promontories of wrack-draped rock. The net is shoved along in front of the prawner so that the wooden boom flushes the prawns out of the sand and into the net. Sometimes very good catches are taken by this method.

Drop-Netting

When the water is coloured by stirred-up sand or mud, or is murky with silt being brought down an estuary after heavy rain, it is possible to use a baited drop-net with excellent results. This is a pouch-shaped net, usually with a ½-inch mesh, laced to a metal hoop of approximately 20 inches diameter. The baited net is lowered to the bottom by means of a rope and bridle (see Fig. 28).

Nowadays shop-bought drop-nets come in a variety of sizes and lightweight materials, but for reasons of cheapness and catching qualities I still favour the traditional home-made net of proofed cotton or nylon laced to a heavy, fast-sinking metal hoop.

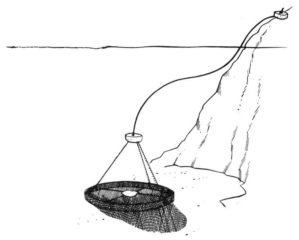

Fig. 28   Drop-net being used from a rock position

However, anglers who have to travel a considerable distance to their fishing will probably prefer one of the modern lightweight designs made of fine-meshed wire net on a thin wire hoop. Besides being easier to carry, this type of drop-net dries very quickly after use and does not corrode the car boot by dripping saltwater during the drive home.

The drop-net is usually baited with a fish head or similar offering. A chunk of mackerel is excellent, because its oily flesh emits an attractive underwater scent trail that travels for a considerable distance. Similarly, a farmer friend of mine reckons there's nothing to beat a piece of skinned rabbit that has been buried in an airtight tin for a week!

The fact of the matter is that prawns are scavengers, and will be attracted to almost any sort of dead flesh.

The most efficient way to attach the bait is to stretch two lengths of twine across the hoop so that they cross at right angles in the centre. The bait is tied to where the lengths of twine intersect.

The art of drop-netting for prawns lies in knowing just where to lower your nets. Places to look for are sheltered muddy-bottomed gullies and pools flanked by weed-draped rocks. The net is lowered to the bottom and allowed to lie there undisturbed for several minutes.

After the necessary time has elapsed, the net should be hauled up quickly and steadily without any preliminary fumbling with the rope.

Prawning with baited drop-nets can be carried on successfully from a wide variety of vantage points, such as tide-exposed reefs, harbour walls, old stone slipways, estuary revetments, stone breakwaters – and, of course, from a small boat working close inshore over a suitable reef.

It is essentially a lazier method of prawning than using a hand-net because the fisherman uses a bait to attract his quarry instead of wading around in search of the prawns.

Prawn Pots
The dinghy angler who lives on a suitable stretch of rocky coast can often provide himself with a regular supply of live prawns for bait by setting one or two prawn pots.

Various designs of prawn pot are used around different parts of the coast, but the majority may be likened to a small cube-shaped lobster pot. Constructed from a metal or wooden framework, and covered with ½-inch mesh netting, the pot is equipped with two or three funnel-shaped entrances and a door for baiting-up and removing the catch (see Fig. 29). A wooden-framed pot will, of course, need to be well weighted with a concrete base.

54

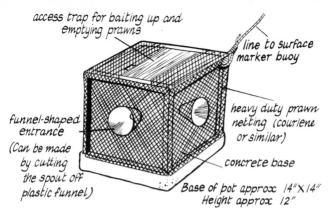

Fig. 29   A prawn pot

The pot entrances can be made by cutting the spout end off a plastic tunnel so as to leave an aperture of about 1 inch diameter. This is large enough to allow big prawns to enter the pot, but small enough to exclude the majority of bait-robbing shore and swimming crabs.

The pots should be set in an area that is known to be rich in prawns, and for best results they should be baited each evening and cleared fairly early in the morning.

Baiting Up

There are several methods of baiting up with prawns, depending on whether they are to be used alive or dead.

For many of our less discerning species of fish, such as pouting, wrasse, gurnards and thornback rays, a dead (but reasonably fresh) prawn makes almost as good a bait as a live one. But if you are mainly interested in catching pollack or big reef bass, then you will do much better by using a plump, freshly-caught prawn that is still alive and kicking.

Light float fishing with a live prawn can be a very good method of catching bass and pollack, and is particularly rewarding when shore fishing from a rocky vantage point or harbour wall; or while dinghy fishing towards late evening in a shallow rocky cove.

Another very killing dinghy fishing method for bass is to lower the anchor quietly and driftline a live prawn so that it swims close to the fringe of a weedy reef, or just outside the entrance to a rocky gully.

To present a live prawn so that it looks as natural as possible, it is usually best to pass the hook upwards through the second or third segment in front of the tail; although some anglers prefer to pass the hook through from side to side.

Fig. 30   Baiting with live prawn

To minimise the risk of fish biting short, and leaving the tail-end of the prawn still attached to the hook, it is essential to keep the terminal tackle as light as possible. The hook should be fine in the wire, with a round bend, and about size 1 or 2.

Although dead prawns also make a very useful bait for the general run of rock-haunting sea fish, they do not have the same appeal as live prawns for bass. Therefore, when using a dead prawn on a driftline, it often helps if the bait is given some movement to make it appear more lively.

This can be done by raising and lowering the rod-tip; or by reeling in for a few yards occasionally, and then allowing the bait to drift away again on the tide.

Incidentally, when using a dead bait, you may find that better results are obtained by inserting the hook in the region of the prawn's mouth, then threading it down until the point emerges near the thorax.

While on the subject of deadbaiting with prawns, it is worth mentioning that I have often used the discarded heads of boiled prawns as bait, and with this 'debris' from the tea table have caught many good bags of black bream — not to mention the inevitable pouting and wrasse.

Keeping Prawns Alive

For the boat angler the simplest method of keeping prawns alive is to place them in a floating wooden courge as soon as possible after they have been caught. One must take care when opening the lid of the courge, however, otherwise some of your hard-won bait may jump out and regain their freedom!

Keeping prawns alive is not quite so simple when shore fishing, but a damp sack or a ventilated bait box filled with damp seaweed will keep them lively for several hours provided you do not leave them exposed to strong sunshine or heavy rain.

A supply of prawns can also be kept alive for two or three days at home in an old porcelain or earthenware sink filled with freshly collected sea water. If an aquarium air pump is used to oxygenate the water, they can be kept alive for considerably longer.

Making a Drop-Net

Although most seaside tackle shops sell drop-nets, they are quite expensive items. However, it is possible to make your own net quite cheaply, as shown in the accompanying illustrations.

Fig. 31 (a) Making a drop-net. To prevent the netting being damaged by rust, the metal hoop is first covered with tightly wound strips of plastic cut from an old fertilizer sack.

The hoop for your drop-net should be about 18 to 22 inches in diameter. Larger ones are awkward to carry over slippery rocks, and seldom catch any more prawns. If a blacksmith still operates in your district, he will make up a hoop quite cheaply. Failing that, your best plan would be to bend the hoop into shape yourself from 3/8-inch mild steel rod, and then get the ends welded at a local car body repair shop.

Rust soon damages netting, so the hoop must be sheathed with tightly wound strips of strong plastic. For this I use 3-inch-wide strips cut from an old 1 cwt plastic fertilizer sack. (NOTE: Hoops made from old bicycle wheel rims are NOT recommended. They quickly rust away in salt water.)

The next job is to attach the netting, which should have a ½-inch mesh. Rot-proof nylon netting will prove cheapest in the long run, even though it is slightly more expensive to buy in the first place. It should be laced to the hoop with nylon twine, using the marline hitch shown in Fig. 31(c).

Fig. 31 (b)   The netting is attached to the hoop, using the marline hitch

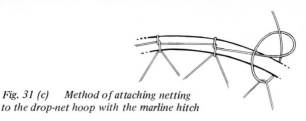

Fig. 31 (c)   Method of attaching netting
to the drop-net hoop with the marline hitch

Be sure to knot the lacing securely after every three turns, so that if the twine frays through against a rock, only a few inches of netting will work loose on the hoop. This lacing will also keep the plastic sheathing firmly in position on the hoop.

I find it easier to shape the netting *after* it has been laced to the hoop. Ideally, the netting should hang down in a neat pouch-shaped bag about 9 - 15 inches deep, depending on the diameter of the hoop. Remember, though, that the depth of the net will tend to decrease as you lace up the bottom and side seams, so when making your first net I suggest you cut the netting about five or six inches deeper than at first appears necessary.

Use nylon twine when lacing together the edges of net. Thread the twine through every mesh, and knot it securely at every alternate mesh.

Incidentally, if you experience difficulty in buying prawn netting at your local tackle shop, it can be purchased by mail order from Bridport-Gundry Ltd., Netmakers, of Bridport, Dorset, who will supply a catalogue and price list on receipt of a large stamped-addressed envelope. However, it should be noted that only standard-sized bundles of prawn netting (sufficient to make *several* drop-nets) can be supplied in this way.

Your drop-net is now ready to be fitted with its rope and bridle. Thin courlene line, which combines lightness with quick-drying properties, is ideal for this purpose. Mark off three equidistant points around the circumference of the hoop, and attach the main length of courlene line at one of these points.

The length of this main line will depend on where you intend to use the net. On a high pier or harbour wall you will naturally need a long rope, but when prawning from tide-pool rocks a long rope can be a dangerous encumbrance.

To complete the three-point bridle attachment, tie in a separate 5ft length of *thinner* line about 20 inches up the main line, leaving two ends of equal length hanging free. Attach these ends to the remaining two marked points on the hoop, making minor adjustments to ensure that the drop-net hangs evenly as shown.

Now slide a small circular net cork down the main line until it comes to rest above the bridle knot; then tie another stop knot above the cork to hold it in position. Attach another cork float to the end of the main line to provide a marker in the event of the line slipping into the water accidentally.

Finally, stretch two lengths of twine at right angles across the mouth of the hoop. You can then tie the bait to the point where these two lengths of twine cross.

Some people tie the bait in the bottom of the net, but this is a mistake. Not only does this method catch less prawns; it may also cause a conger to tear a hole through the net in its efforts to get at the bait!

Mussels

Although the Common Mussel (*Mytilus edulis*) makes a really excellent bait for a wide variety of sea fish, and is widely distributed all around our coasts, there are many areas (particularly in the south) where it is almost completely ignored by the local sea anglers.

This is probably due to the fact that some skill and 'know-how' are required in order to extract this bivalve mollusc from its strong and tightly-closed shell. Also, care must be taken when baiting up with the soft flesh if your offering is to remain on the hook when casting.

Large mussels, about three inches or more in length, are the ones most favoured for hook bait, and these are usually found near the limits of low spring tides, adhering in tight-packed colonies to suitably situated reefs and longshore rocks, stone harbour walls, jetty piles, pier stanchions, mooring hawsers, and also in smaller individual clusters among the gravelly stones and tidal rocks forming the shores of sea-lochs and estuaries.

Smaller mussels can often be gathered at less favourable states of the tide, but those under about two inches in length are not really worth using as bait — except when fishing for mullet with a very small hook.

Mussels are found around most suitable stretches of the European coastline, from the Mediteranean to the north of Scotland, and in the Baltic.

Opening Mussels

There is a knack in opening mussels so that the soft interior flesh can be presented on the hook neatly and efficiently. First of all, you must equip yourself with a suitable knife, and my own favourite tool for the job is an old stainless steel table knife with half the blade snapped off and the remaining half reshaped on a grindstone to the dimensions shown in Fig. 32.

To open a mussel, hold if firmly between the thumb and first two fingers of your left hand, with the 'straight' edge of the shell facing towards you.

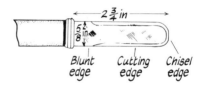

Fig. 32   A useful tool for opening mussels, made by grinding down the stub of an old table-knife

The knife, of course, is held in the other hand, and although it is gripped by the handle, some additional control is obtained by pressing the thumb and forefinger against the blunt edges of the blade.

Begin by scraping the knife blade along the edge of the shell at the point marked A in Fig. 33(a). This will remove any traces of the byssus threads that originally anchored the mussel to its rock or harbour pile, and underneath will be revealed a tiny gap where the two halves of the shell fit together. Into this gap you can insert the chisel-edged tip of the knife.

As soon as the tip of the blade has penetrated between the two halves of the shell, the knife blade

Fig. 33 (a).   Open mussel by working the knife around the blunt end of the shell; then reverse direction towards pointed end

Fig 33 (b)   The opened mussel with the flesh lying unbroken in the lower half of the shell

should be slanted upwards, and then carefully worked further in with a wiggling motion so that it passes between the flesh of the mollusc and the inside of the shell.

The blade (still slanting upwards) is then worked sideways around the blunt end of the shell. After rounding the end of the shell you will feel something 'give' as the cutting edge of the knife severs the adductor muscle which keeps the shell closed – and then suddenly the two halves of the shell will gape slightly.

The knife is then run back around the shell in the opposite direction as far as the pointed end (C) of the shell. The top half of the shell can then be lifted clear, revealing the fleshy body of the mussel reposing in the other half.

It is now a simple matter to slice (with the cutting edge of the knife) and scoop (with the rounded tip of the blade) the mussel from this remaining half of the shell.

Baiting Up

Because mussel is a rather soft bait it is really best suited for boat and pier fishing, or for those steep-to beach and

62

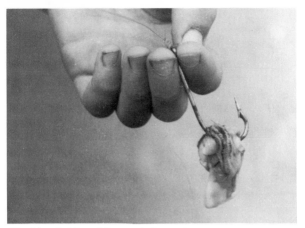

Fig. 34   Baiting with mussel. (Larger baits can be obtained by mounting two or three mussels on a single hook.)

rock situations where only short casts are needed in order to reach the fish. Forceful long-distance casting is liable to cause the bait to fly off the hook; although tying the bait on with a few turns of soft wool will reduce this risk, and at the same time helps to prevent fish from sucking off the bait without falling foul of the hook.

Hooks used with mussel should be fine in the wire and free of rust. Sliced shank hooks must be avoided; otherwise the bait will slide up the shank during the cast and remain there, trapped by the barbs, with the result that you will get plenty of bites but very few hooked fish.

When baiting up, the point of the hook should first be inserted through the dark-coloured protrusion, often referred to as the 'tongue' or 'neb', which is situated between the two lobes of the mussel. After emerging from the side of the mussel the hook is twisted and inserted once again through an area of comparatively firm flesh situated near where the lobes are 'hinged' together; after which the bait is turned and the hook passed through the gristly disc of muscle.

Depending on the size of the hook, and the species of fish expected, several mussels can be threaded one after the other on a single hook to provide a really generous

63

bait. For big cod I would suggest four or five mussels on a long-shanked 4/0 Aberdeen; for codling, bass and plaice one could use three mussels on a size 2/0; whilst one or two mussels are usually sufficient to tempt flounders, bream, whiting, pouting, etc.

Mussels are normally opened a few hours before they are required for use, so that they have time to dry and firm up in the fresh air. If this is done at home before setting off on a fishing trip it is a good idea to spread the prepared baits on some sheets of absorbent newspaper.

On the other hand, if you have to open your mussels while actually fishing you may like to make use of an idea which was passed on to me by a Yorkshire sea angler. He has fitted a piece of foam plastic into the bottom of his bait bucket, and this allows the water to soak away from his freshly shelled mussels, making them much easier to handle when baiting up.

As an alternative, some anglers recommend that mussels should be gently heated in a little water until their shells open; but although this saves some knife-work and makes the flesh firmer, it also seems to take away some of the attractiveness of the bait. However, it is said that a few drops of pilchard oil, sprinkled over the mussels while they are still warm, helps to overcome this difficulty.

Yet another popular dodge which I have found particularly useful is to tip a mussel-baited hook with a medium-sized lugworm or small piece of squid tentacle. A cocktail bait along these lines not only doubles the interest value of the bait, but also helps to prevent sly-biting fish from pulling off the soft mussel flesh.

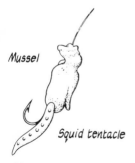

*Fig. 35 A tasty cocktail –
a mussel combined with a squid
tentacle*

Storing Mussels

Mussels can be kept alive for several weeks if placed in a clean hessian sack suspended from a quay wall or boat mooring. If this is not possible, they can be kept for several days in a sea-damped sack with a quantity of wet, freshly gathered seaweed. The sack should, of course, be kept in a cool, shady place.

Another method which I have used successfully is to keep a supply of mussels in an old earthenware sink filled with clean, fresh seawater. If the mussels have been gathered from the shores of an estuary or harbour, it is important to scrub the shells thoroughly to remove all traces of mud before placing them in the storage tank.

Whisking the water vigorously for about a minute twice a day with a flat piece of wood helps to keep it oxygenated, and in this way I have kept mussels alive for over a week. With the help of a small aquarium air pump, and an occasional change of sea water, the storage period can be extended for considerably longer.

It is a pity that mussels are not used by more sea anglers, because they are one of the few saltwater baits that are not threatened by over-exploitation. This is largely due to the mussel's remarkable powers of reproduction, and its ability to colonize an area of shallow water in a remarkably short time.

Just how quickly and efficiently mussels are able to establish themselves was proved in dramatic fashion towards the end of the Second World War when, in the process of liberating the Netherlands from the invading German forces, a breaching of the dykes resulted in much of the Isle of Walcheren disappearing under the waters of the North Sea.

Some twelve months later, when the dykes had been repaired and the land slowly began to reappear as the great pumps did their work, it was found that almost everything had become covered with millions of mussels — roads, field gates, the walls of houses. They even encrusted the branches of the salt-killed trees.

Red and King Ragworms

The term 'ragworm' is used by sea anglers to describe various marine annelids which vary considerably in size, coloration and habitat. However, they all possess a somewhat compressed body, divided into approximately a hundred or more segments, and fringed on either side with bristled centipede-like feet known as parapodia.

So far as the bait-hunter is concerned, ragworms may be divided conveniently into three main groups: Small red Harbour Ragworm of approximately 2 to 3 inches in length; medium-sized reddish or bronzy-hued Ragworm (approximately 3½ to 5 inches); and the large greenish King Ragworm (*Nereis virens*) which attains a length of 12 to 18 inches.

There are also some pale flesh-coloured worms commonly known as White Ragworm, but these are dealt with separately in this book, due mainly to the fact that they favour a different type of habitat.

For the most part ragworms lead an active life, burrowing in mud or muddy gravel, both on the open coast and in sheltered estuaries, sounds and sea lochs. They are present in the inshore shallows as well as on the lower shoreline, but of ourse it is those living between the tide lines that interest the bait-digger. The majority of these bait species have a wide distribution range which extends from the Mediterranean, along the Atlantic coast of Europe to the English Channel, North Sea and west Baltic.

However, although ragworms spend most of their lives in obscurity, during the mating season many species emerge in dense swarms from their muddy burrows, and then swim upwards to release their eggs and sperm in the inshore shallows. During this reproductive stage, known as the *Heteroneries* the lateral parapodia become enlarged and more paddle-shaped to increase the worm's swimming efficiency.

This mass nuptial swim of the ragworms usually takes place at night, and is the reason why anglers fishing early in the morning for pollack over inshore reefs sometimes find the stomachs of the fish they catch crammed full of ragworm.

Digging

Although most seaside tackle shops sell live ragworms, the demand often exceeds the supply during the peak holiday months. However, in a suitable coastal area an able-bodied angler should experience no difficulty in digging several days' supply for himself during a single low tide.

The type of ragworm likely to be found will depend very largely upon the nature of the shoreline, but digging this bait is nearly always a wet and rather muddy business, so a pair of wellington boots will be required.

You will also need a digging fork with strong, sharp tines. A spade is likely to prove useless, due to the stony, gravelly nature of many ragworm grounds.

The bait-box should be made of wood or plastic (not metal), and be fitted with a close-fitting but ventilated lid. In this sort of container the worms will live for well over a week if kept cool and given a thin layer of coarse sea-damp gritty sand to crawl around in. When it happens to be available, I also spread a few sprigs of coralline weed, plucked fresh and dripping wet from a rock pool, on top of the sand in the bait-box.

Perhaps the most generally useful ragworms are the medium-sized ones. These are fairly widely distributed around our coasts, and are most likely to be found in estuaries, sheltered coves and large natural harbours where the lower shoreline consists of mixed mud and gravel.

On some ragworm grounds it is not unusual to find numerous small flattish boulders lying on the surface of the mud, and if you turn some of these over quickly there is a good chance that you will surprise a large ragworm lying underneath. You must grab the worm quickly, because it will begin to squirm head-first down its hole with remarkable speed.

Take hold of the worm near its head if you possibly can, because if gripped at the other end it is liable to leave you holding an inch or so of its tail, while the rest of it disappears swiftly into the ground. Although this bit of tail will probably be too thin and short to be much use, you may decide to retain it in case bait runs short. In which event you may be somewhat startled to find the tail still wriggling around in the bait-box a day or two later!

On a few localized parts of the coast, notably in the Solent area, you are likely to come across the big King Ragworm. Huge quantities are collected by commercial bait-diggers for distribution to tackle shops on other parts of the coast where this type of bait does not occur naturally.

The novice sea angler, on handling one of these big ragworm for the first time, may be rather alarmed to see a pair of small horn-shaped 'nippers' shooting in and out aggressively on either side of the creature's mouth. These can inflict quite a painful bite, but they will be unable to do any harm provided you grip the worm firmly behind its head, using your forefinger and thumb.

By way of contrast to the large King Ragworm, there's the small red Harbour Ragworm. It is found in vast numbers all around our coasts wherever there are harbours, creeks or estuaries containing thick, glutinous mud. No particular skill is required to dig these worms, and indeed when I was a boy we used to wade into the mud and scoop the worms out with our hands.

Collecting harbour rag is usually a messy business whichever way you do it — but they make a good bait for mullet, and when bunched on the hook will also take bass and flatfish.

Baiting Up

The usual method of baiting up with medium-sized ragworm is to insert the hook-point in the mouth, and then thread the worm carefully around the bend and up the shank of the hook as far as the eye. When the worm is a fairly long one, some anglers slide the head of the worm over the hook-eye and an inch or so up the nylon hook dropper. The point of the hook is brought out again lower down the worm's body to leave about two inches of the tail dangling free.

The job of baiting up will be made much more easy if a clean, rust-free hook is used — fine in the wire, and preferably with a round bend. Also, a hook with a sliced shank is helpful, as the protruding barbs on the shank keep the worm neatly in position when casting.

Ragworm presented in this way will appeal to a wide

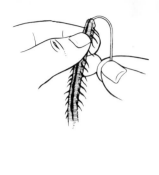

Fig 36 (a)   The point of a long-shanked hook is inserted into the worm's head

Fig. 36 (b)   The bend and shank of the hook are threaded carefully through the upper half of the ragworm's body, and the point is then brought out again to leave the tail dangling.

variety of fish, including bass, pollack, flatfish, sea bream, pouting, wrasse, gurnard, etc. They can be used when groundfishing, float fishing, driftlining and spinning; while in many areas a ragworm is the favourite choice when fishing for flounders with a baited spoon.

Very large King Ragworm can, if necessary, be cut into two portions, and each half of the worm threaded on the hook in the manner just described. Alternatively, in areas where King Rag are easily obtainable, and there is no compelling need to economize, the whole worm may be used as a trolling bait for bass, mounted on a tandem hook arrangement behind a revolving silver-coloured spoon or spinner.

Baiting up with small Harbour Ragworm calls for a little more care because the worms are rather soft when first dug out of the mud, and will disintegrate if threaded incorrectly on the hook. If not required for immediate use, the worms can be made firmer by leaving them for a day or two on several thicknesses of absorbent newspaper. It is best to place the paper in the bottom of a large seed box, or something similar, so that the edges of the paper curl upwards to prevent the worms from

69

straying. Do NOT attempt to hasten the drying out process by leaving the worms in the sun — instead, be sure to keep them in a cool, shady place.

During this storage period the worms will squirm together into a tight-packed bunch. When required for use they should be transferred into a bait-box along with a liberal quantity of dry sawdust or garden peat. This, coupled with some gentle 'teasing out' with your fingers, will encourage them to disentangle themselves.

It is essential to use a straight-eyed or spade-ended fine-wire hook when baiting up with small harbour rag. Several worms are bunched on each hook, and when baiting up with the first worm the point of the hook is inserted into the side of the head and brought out again about half an inch further down the body, leaving the remainder of the worm dangling. The worm is then slid up the hook shank and over the eye (or spade end) to rest on the nylon dropper.

The second worm is dealt with in the same way, and then slid up the hook shank to just below the eye. Finally, the top half-inch of a third worm is threaded around the lower part of the hook to leave just the point and barb protruding, and the tail dangling free.

Bunched on the hook in this way, small Harbour Ragworm make a good bait for bass, flounders, pollack and mullet, depending on the size of the hook. They can be used with most fishing methods, including legering, float fishing, and the various applications of the baited spoon.

Rock Pool Eels

Young freshwater and conger eels, ranging in length from about 4 to 7 inches, make excellent baits for bass and pollack. They are often to be found at low tide, hiding under small boulders and trailing fronds of wrack.

Sheltered estuaries and inlets are usually the most rewarding places to look for them, but shallow drying reefs on the open coast can also be productive. Pay special attention to those boulders which are small enough to be overturned quickly by hand, and which are lying on fairly hard damp ground or bedrock (not soft mud) so that there are gaps underneath just large enough to conceal your quarry.

A small eel is a very slippery and elusive customer, and for this reason it's a good idea to equip yourself with an old table-fork, so that the prongs can be brought down quickly to hold the eel before it has a chance to disappear again under another boulder or clump of weed.

A small live eel, hooked lightly through the back an inch or two behind the head, makes an excellent float fishing bait for bass and pollack.

Eels about 6 to 7 inches long can also be used as trolling baits for the same two species. When required for the latter purpose the point of a long-shanked hook is inserted into the mouth of a dead eel and brought out again through the underside about one-third of the way down the body. The head and upper part of the eel should be threaded carefully up the hook shank until the hook eye disappears into the eel's mouth. A turn of fine nylon line is then knotted tightly around the snout of the eel to prevent the body sliding back down the hook shank.

This can be a very killing natural trolling bait in those coastal areas where sandeels are not readily available, and on the Dorset coast, when dinghy trolling over inshore rock marks, I have taken many pollack on this bait to well over 10lb.

Small rock pool eels can be kept alive for several days in a plastic bucket partly filled with damp seaweed. Alternatively they can be kept for considerably longer periods in the type of aerated livebait tank described in the section on Sandeels.

Butterfish

The Butterfish, or Spotted Gunnel (*Pholis gunnellus*) is another slippery little fish which dwells on weedy, boulder-littered shores. Attaining a length of about 7 or 8 inches, it has a mottled reddish-brown eel-like body which is marked with a row of dark spots along the base of the dorsal fin. These dark spots have a distinctive pale outer ring.

Butterfish are most likely to be found fairly low down on the shoreline, hiding under boulders or dense clumps of weed, where they take refuge in preference to the rock pools when the tide recedes.

A dead butterfish threaded up a large long-shanked hook makes a useful spinning bait for bass and pollack. Alternatively, in areas where sand runs in close alongside rocks, it can be used very effectively as a bottom fishing bait — especially if cast out and then retrieved slowly in short spasmodic jerks.

Piddocks

These bivalve molluscs conceal themselves from predators by boring into soft rocks, such as chalk, sandstones, blue lias and indurated clays, along the lower shoreline and in shallow water.

Several species of piddock inhabit the shores of Britain and western Europe, but the most useful one for bait is the widely distributed Common Piddock (*Pholas dactylus*) which attains a length of up to six inches. Due to the considerable length of its siphons, it is capable of excavating a burrow almost twice as long as its shell.

The best time to search for piddocks is during a low spring tide, and to excavate them from their burrows you will need a hammer and chisel. The holes made by the piddocks will be about ½ to ¾ inch in diameter at the entrance, and a rock inhabited by a colony of piddocks looks rather like a huge lump of fossilized Gruyere cheese!

To avoid unnecessary damage to the host rock it is advisable to chisel open the burrows individually. Before attacking a burrow, however, you'll be wise to check that it is occupied. This can be done by tapping with the hammer close to the bole, and watching for the tell-tale spurt of water as the piddock involuntarily retreats deeper into its dwelling.

Fig. 37   A piddock partly excavated from its burrow in a tide-exposed limestone rock

When exposed to the light of day the piddock will be found to have a very thin and brittle shell, so it must be handled carefully if you wish to keep it alive for any length of time. Certainly there's no difficulty in removing the shell when preparing this bait for the hook. The siphon is the firmest part, and stays on the hook well when distance casting.

During the chiselling out process the mollusc will probably have contracted its siphon tube, but this can be stretched out again to something approaching its full length prior to threading it on a fine-wire, round-bend hook.

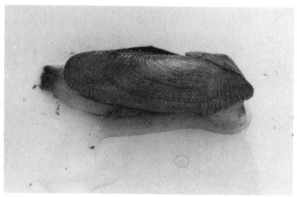

Fig. 38 (a)   Piddock after being chiselled out of the rock

Fig. 38 (b)   Baiting with piddock

One rather unusual characteristic of the piddock is that it possesses special glands which secrete a luminous slime, so that the creature emits a strange greenish-blue glow in the dark. This probably increases its efficiency as a night fishing bait, and in the West Country quite a few sea anglers use piddocks with very good results when fishing for bass after dark on bouldery stretches of shoreline. They are also relished by cod, whiting, flatfish and wrasse.

Piddocks can be kept alive for several days if placed in a plastic bucket partly filled with clean sea water. Storage time will be increased if the water is changed every second day.

Part Three
Baits from the Open Sea

Fish Baits

Mackerel, Herring and Pilchards

There can be few hook offerings more generally attractive to big fish than a piece of herring, mackerel or pilchard. These three fish baits are particularly useful because their flesh emits an attractive oily scent-trail into the water, which acts on any predatory fish swimming down-tide like the 'Cookhouse' bugle call on a troop of hungry Boy Scouts!

For maximum success, however, the length, shape and thickness of your fish strip must suit the species you are seeking. If possible, it should also move or flutter temptingly in the flow of tide. These are important points which many sea anglers, particularly beginners, tend to overlook.

Let's assume, for example, that you are cutting up a medium-sized mackerel for hook bait. First and foremost, the knife must be razor-sharp. It is best to keep a thin-bladed filleting knife specially for cutting up bait, and to have a second stout-bladed knife for the more rugged jobs like cutting hooks out of gristly jaws, or slicing the wings off rays.

The first part of the job is to slice a fillet from each side of the mackerel, and whether you begin cutting your fillet from the head end of the fish, or at the tail-end, is purely a matter of personal preference. My own method is to lay the mackerel on its side on the cutting board, holding the head with my left hand. The knife blade is then slipped under the pectoral fin to lift it out of the way, and a cut made straight down immediately behind the root of the fin until I feel the blade touch the backbone. The narrow blade is then turned horizontally with its edge towards the tail – and using a slicing movement the blade is run smoothly along the backbone until it finally severs the fillet completely at the root of the tail. The fillet will, of course, taper off to a point as you reach the tail.

The mackerel is now turned over, and a fillet removed from the other side in exactly the same way.

The advantage of this method is that throughout the operation one is cutting AWAY from the hand that is holding the mackerel on the board. NEVER cut towards your 'holding' hand because this can have dire consequences, especially when cutting up bait in a boat that is pitching violently in a choppy sea!

For those who prefer to begin filleting their bait at the tail-end it is simply a matter of holding the fish by the root of the tail for the first inch or two of the cut, and then transferring one's grip further up the body as the blade travels towards the head.

After removing the fillets from an extra large mackerel it may be necessary to place each fillet skin

Fig. 39.   Cutting up fish baits should be done with a razor-sharp knife. Here an angler is slicing fillets from some freshly-caught mackerel. Note that for safety reasons, the direction of cut is away from the hand holding the fish's head. The knife-blade is sliding along the mackerel's backbone.

side downwards on the cutting board, so that any unwanted 'high spots' of flesh can be trimmed off to leave you with a neat and fairly thin slice.

Figures 40(a), (b) and (c) show some methods of cutting up a fillet into strip baits of varying shapes and sizes to suit different species of fish. If you are seeking sizeable bottom-feeding fish, such as turbot, thornback rays, cod, large wreck pollack or deep-sea ling, you should divide the fillet lengthways into two long, narrow strips, as shown in Fig. 40(a). You can then shape the

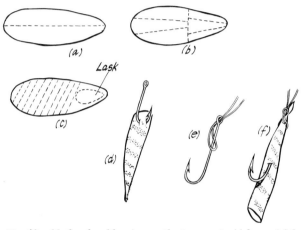

Fig. 40   Mackerel and herring are the two most widely used fish baits, and shown here are some methods which enable the strips of flesh to be presented to their best advantage
(a) A whole fillet, sliced from the side of the fish, is divided down the middle to provide long, tapering baits with a superficial resemblance to a sandeel. Excellent when driftlining for large pollack, ling and cod; or legering for turbot, etc.
(b) and (c) Two methods of cutting up fish baits for smaller species, such as black bream, whiting and other mackerel. For best results, trim off surplus flesh to provide flexible strips about 3/16 inch thick. In method (c) the strip marked 'lask' is the section of tough skin immediately in front on the mackerel's tail. It is mainly used to add some extra attraction to an artificial lure when trolling, and should be cut from the whole mackerel – i.e. before filleting.
(d) Method of baiting with the tapering strips shown in (b).
(e) A hook mounted on a loop-ended nylon dropper allows a long fish strip to be held firmly at its upper end under the tightened loop, as shown in (f).

ends of the two strips so that the final effect resembles the streamlined shape of a sandeel.

The strip baits produced by the methods illustrated in Figs. 40(b) and (c) are better suited for fish which are normally caught on small to medium-sized hooks — say from about size 4 to 2/0.

In Fig. 40(c) the portion marked 'lask' is obtainable only when using a fresh mackerel as bait, and is normally cut from the whole fish — i.e. before filleting. Primarily used when trolling to add extra interest to the hook of an artificial lure, this type of bait should be sliced very thinly with only a little flesh adhering to the skin.

Now let's take another look at those long strip baits shown in Fig. 40(a). As previously mentioned, these can be tapered slightly to imitate the appearance of a sandeel, and when fishing for turbot, pollack and ling it also helps considerably if your bait has an attractive action in the water. To achieve this you must trim the strip so that the flesh attached to the skin is only $\frac{1}{4}$ to $\frac{1}{3}$ of an inch thick, depending on the size of the hook.

There are various ways of attaching a long strip bait to the hook. One method, commonly used in areas where tides are fairly slack, is as follows:

First, insert the hook-point through the tapered end of the strip, which should then be slid up the shank. Next, holding the strip between the forefinger and thumb of your left hand, circle the hook-shank around the strip and thrust the hook point through it again; then repeat the process once more.

On some parts of the coast this is the method used by professional fishermen when baiting up their longlines. It has the advantage of holding the bait firmly on the hook for long periods, and leaves an attractive tail of bait dangling from the bend of a hook.

However, when legering or driftlining in a fast run of tide — over a turbot bank, for example — the twists of bait around the hook shank are liable to make it spin in the water, eventually producing a kinked and tangled trace.

In strong tides, therefore, it is better to leave the strip untwisted. Fortunately, fish tend to bite boldly in fast-moving water, so it is usually safe to present the bait as described.

Alternatively, if the fish are 'biting short', the method shown in Figs. 40(e) and (f) can be used. In this, the hook (preferably one with a turned-down eye) is attached to the trace by means of a loop, and the tapered end of the strip bait is run up the shank and trapped securely in position beneath the loop. The point of the hook is then passed through the strip again, leaving about 2½ inches of bait dangling free. This is a particularly good method of presenting fish baits when driftlining for deep-sea pollack and ling.

So far we have only discussed the use of fish strips and fillets, but is is worth mentioning that a tiny mackerel, commonly referred to as a 'joey', makes a particularly succulent morsel for most predators, including conger, tope, skate, rays, huss, bass, etc.

When legering or driftlining with a dead joey, mount it on the hook so that is is presented to the fish head-first. However, do not overlook the alternative possibility of livebaiting with a lip-hooked joey, because this can be a really killing method for many species, including bass, big reef pollack and turbot.

Likewise, spinning with a dead joey mounted on a spinning flight can provide sport with big bass in areas where sandeels are not available, and will often produce results when the fish refuse to take an artificial lure.

Dead medium-sized mackerel are also often used whole when legering for tope or drifting for shark. The bait should be presented head-first, and this is best done with the help of a baiting needle (see Fig. 24).

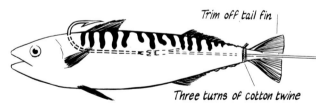

Fig. 41 An efficient method of baiting up for shark with a whole dead mackerel. The hook and stainless steel wire link are threaded through the mackerel with the aid of a baiting needle. The hook point is shown here emerging through the top of the mackerel's head, but some anglers prefer the hook to emerge through the eye-socket. A shark prefers to take the bait head-first.

Another good bait for tope, conger and large bass is the head of a freshly-killed mackerel, ripped off the body so as to leave the guts trailing. The size of hook used will naturally depend on the size of the mackerel head, but to ensure efficient penetration the hook should be large enough to leave the point standing well clear of the bait when it emerges through the top of the head.

It is also worth bearing in mind that fish baits invariably produce their best results when they are fresh-caught from the sea, and still oozing blood and natural oils. This is particularly true of mackerel baits, which are firmer and stay on the hook better when used within an hour or two of capture. Therefore a trolling or feathering session in quest of fresh mackerel is always a worthwhile prelude to any deep-sea fishing trip.

Having caught your bait, keep it as fresh as possible. Don't leave mackerel or cut-up bait strips lying in the sun or they will quickly become soft and useless. Keep them under a clean hessian sack damped at regular intervals with sea water. Or, better still, keep a supply of whole mackerel suspended in a net bag over the side of the boat, so that they are just dipping in the water.

However, don't use this last method when shark fishing with a rubby-dubby trail, or you may suddenly lose your netful of hook bait to a hungry shark. It happened to me once – while fishing in a 13ft dinghy!

Herrings for use as hook bait can be presented whole, as fillets, or cut into strips in much the same way as mackerel. The best herrings to use are fresh-caught ones obtained direct from local netsmen, but chilled (not frozen) herrings purchased from a fishmonger are also accepted readily by the majority of sea fish. When shop-bought herrings have to be stored overnight prior to use as bait the following day, it is a good idea to sprinkle them liberally with coarse cooking salt. This toughens the flesh and makes it easier to cut up and mount on the hook neatly.

Pilchards were at one time netted in their millions in West Country waters, and in those days this was the favourite bait among Cornish anglers fishing for conger, ling, shark, bass, skate, rays, turbot, brill, cod, whiting, pollack, haddock, etc. Unfortunately, in recent years the
80

West Country pilchard fisheries have suffered a serious decline, and this bait is now often difficult to obtain where it was once so plentiful. However, when available it is still as killing as ever – due mainly to its rich oil content. The fish can be used whole, as fillets, or cut into strips by the methods already suggested for mackerel and herring.

Pilchard oil (extracted by pressing the fish) is sold by most seaside tackle shops, and makes a valuable additive for many saltwater groundbait mixtures. When smeared on to an otherwise second-rate hook bait it will often add considerably to its attractiveness.

The Cutting Board

This should be rinsed or sponged clean at regular intervals during a fishing session to remove slippery blood and slime. It is difficult, if not impossible, to cut neat baits on a slippery board, and in rough sea conditions it also makes the job more dangerous.

Any off-cut of close-grained timber, about 24 inches by 18 inches, will serve as a cutting board. Do not varnish the board because this will make it more slippery. For the same reason I have no liking for cutting boards made from Formica and similar shiny-surfaced materials – even though they are easier to keep clean.

Freezing

Generally speaking, oily fish do not freeze very well. In times of summer glut, many sea anglers freeze down quantities of mackerel for use as bait during the winter months when fresh mackerel are not available. The experiment is rarely a success because thawed-out mackerel flesh is soft and does not stay on the hook well when casting. It is also very vulnerable to attacks by crabs and tiny pouting; yet does not seem to be very attractive to larger fish.

However, de-frosted mackerel flesh, pounded to a mushy pulp, makes a useful groundbait for mullet and many other species of fish.

Sprats

These small silvery-hued fish are netted in large quantities around many parts of the coast during late autumn and winter. Rich in oil, they make a most attractive bait for whiting, cod, dabs, flounders and late-season bass, pollack and turbot. Sprats obtained direct from local netsmen are likely to make the best baits, being fresher and firmer-fleshed, and therefore easier to keep on the hook.

Sprats purchased from the fishmonger are easier to deal with if covered with salt overnight. This toughens up the flesh.

When fishing for fairly large fish, such as cod and conger, several sprats can be fished whole on a large round-bend hook. The simplest method of doing this is to pass the hook-point through the eye-sockets, so that the bunched sprats hang tail downwards from the bend of the hook.

For large whiting, bass or pollack I like to use a whole sprat on a fine-wire, long-shanked 4/0 hook. For reasons that will be made clear very shortly, the hook is attached to the nylon trace or dropper by means of a loop.

The hook point is passed through the sprat from side to side exactly one full shank-length from the root of

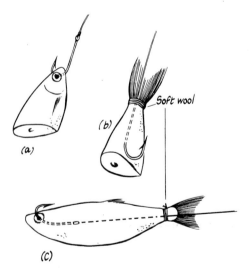

Fig. 42   Some methods of baiting with sprats. Method (a) is best suited to boat and pier fishing, where distance casting is not called for.

the tail. By positioning the hook carefully in this way, it is then possible to trap the root of the tail under the nylon loop, where it passes through the hook-eye. The advantage of this method is that it holds the sprat securely when beachcasting.

As a general rule, however, sprat baits are mostly used for boat fishing. The whole sprat method just described is particularly effective when presented on light driftline tackle from an anchored boat.

When fishing for medium-sized whiting, flatfish, etc., sprats can be filleted and the whole fillets presented in the same way as small strips of mackerel or herring. In the case of very large sprats, it may be necessary to divide the fillets lengthways down the middle before baiting up.

Sardines
These are, in fact, young pilchards. They are hardly ever used as bait in British waters, but for sea anglers in Portugal, Spain, Gibraltar and many other countries in southern Europe and North Africa sardines are probably the most widely used of all saltwater fishing baits. Suspended by their eye sockets in bunches, in the manner described for sprats, they will take a wide variety of deep-sea fish, including large grouper, moray eels, etc.

When fishing from rock positions and harbour walls, sardines (either whole or cut into portions) are also an excellent float fishing bait. Catches are usually much improved in this sort of fishing if some of the sardines are used as groundbait — the usual method being to crumble the tiny fish between one's fingers before throwing the pieces into the swim at regular intervals.

Non-oily Fish Baits
In addition to the oily fish we have just discussed, the following non-oily fish can also be used very successfully as baits for certain kinds of specialized fishing:

Pouting. A small dead pouting is one of the best baits available for conger, and so is a fillet taken from a large pouting. Tope, too, will often accept a whole fresh-caught pouting, although I would not rate this bait so highly for tope as a fresh mackerel or sea bream.

A small live pouting is a first-class float or driftlining bait for bass. For this method of fishing I normally use a treble hook, with one of the hooks passed sideways through the nose of the bait.

Alternatively, when legering from a harbour breakwater or rock position, it is possible to catch big bass by baiting up with a dead pouting, provided it is made slightly buoyant by injecting it with air from a hypodermic syringe.

Strips of pouting are yet another useful bass bait – as witness the case of two Folkestone anglers, Clive Wire and Martin Myland, who fished right through a stormy night on Dungeness Beach. Baiting up with strips of pouting, they caught fifteen bass between them. The largest bass, captured by Clive, weighed 10lb 12oz.

Pouting baits can be particularly useful when fishing from a beach that is swarming with small pouting and poor-cod. These pesky little bait-robbers are capable of quickly stripping a hook of all the usual offerings such as ragworm, mackerel strips, herring, peeler crab, sandeels or lug. The only bait they don't seem to relish is another pouting!

Young Pollack and Coalfish. Tiny pollack and coalfish, ranging from about 3 to 5 inches in length, often swarm in the vicinity of harbour walls and rocks, and can be easily caught on small ragworm-baited hooks and tiny spinners. Presented live on light float or driftline tackle, these small fry make an excellent bait for bass and larger pollack. Use a fine-wire hook, and pass the point through the lips. Alternatively, when float fishing, snick the hook lightly through the back just in front of the dorsal fin.

Sea Bream. Small dead red and black bream make an acceptable bait for tope. They should be presented head-first on the hook with the aid of a baiting needle, in the manner recommended when baiting with whole mackerel (see Fig. 41).

Larger bream, after being scaled, can be filleted and used as bait for conger. Also, small strips of black bream flesh will often be taken by other black bream when there is a shortage of more orthodox baits. Anointing the strips with pilchard oil helps to make this bait more attractive.

Wrasse. A small live wrasse, ranging from about 3 to 6 inches in length, makes a really excellent bait for big bass. Normally, when fishing from a rock position or harbour breakwater, the bait is hooked through the back and suspended below sliding float tackle. However, this bait is also very killing when driftlined from an anchored boat in the vicinity of an inshore reef or rocky headland. These useful little bait fish can often be caught at the fishing position on a separate set of tackle carrying small hooks.

Sand Smelts. Can be obtained and used as bass baits in the same way as the small wrasse mentioned in the preceding paragraph. When float fishing the hook should be passed through the back just behind the first dorsal fin. Smelts also make excellent spinning and trolling baits for bass and pollack, and when using these methods they can be presented on the hook in much the same way as a sandeel.

Garfish. Although not often used as a hook bait, strips cut from the side of a freshly-caught garfish are well worth using as a substitute for mackerel when the latter are in short supply. When used on light float or driftline tackle, strips of garfish flesh are taken eagerly by mackerel and other garfish. At the same time small chopped up pieces of garfish can be used as groundbait with very good effect.

When legering with larger strips of garfish from a boat I have also had conger and thornback rays, and on one memorable occasion I caught a 24½ lb turbot on a long strip of garfish cut from the tail section to resemble a sandeel.

Livebaiting

Small wrasse and sand smelts intended for use as livebaits can be kept alive for long periods if placed immediately after capture in a plastic bucket of sea water that is aerated by a battery-powered aquarium air pump. Further details of this type of livebait container will be found in the chapter dealing with sandeels.

Squid and Cuttlefish

Both Squid and Cuttlefish are molluscs which have attained a very high level of evolutionary development. Unlike so many other molluscs, they do not have an external shell. Instead, the shell is represented by an internal limey bone, or 'pen', and this adaptation enables these creatures to lead a free-swimming life in the open sea, and when the need arises they are capable of a considerable display of speed and agility.

They possess a streamlined sac-like body, and a head equipped with large eyes and a horny beaked mouth. This mouth is encircled by ten sucker-studded tentacles, two of which are much longer than the other eight. These long tentacles are used to 'lassoo' small fish and crustacean prey, which are then torn to pieces by the beaked mouth.

Squid and cuttle are able to move through the water in two different ways. Normally they swim in fairly leisurely fashion by rippling their fins; but when danger threatens, or some other emergency arises which calls for speed, they discharge a powerful stream of water from an exhalant siphon which sends them shooting backwards. Jet propulsion, in fact.

When pursued by an enemy, squid and cuttle are also able to discharge a cloud of dark-coloured 'ink', or sepia, which billows out behind them like a smoke screen. This effectively covers their retreat, and confuses the enemy so that it usually abandons the chase.

Squid appear to be slightly more attractive to most predatory fish than cuttlefish, and therefore they are marginally the better hook bait. Among many sea anglers, in fact, squid is the most widely used of all winter baits. This is very largely due to the fact that squid flesh retains its attractive properties after quite long periods in the domestic freezer, and therefore winter bait supplies can be virtually guaranteed when rough weather and inconvenient tides make it impossible to gather fresh baits.

I recall the time, back in the 1950s, when the seine netsmen on my local stretch of the Dorset coast, when shooting their nets for the inshore mackerel shoals, would occasionally haul in vast numbers of 'useless' squid. Any anglers who happened to be fishing on the beach nearby would then be invited to help themselves to as many as they could use for bait before the remainder were shovelled back into the sea.

Nowadays, of course, the delicious eating qualities of squid are more widely appreciated in this country, and they command a high price in the fish markets. Consequently, this very useful bait can be rather expensive when purchased from a fishmonger or seaside tackle shop. Fortunately, however, there are occasions when the boat angler is able to catch a good supply for himself on rod and line, and these will keep for many months if frozen or salted down within a few hours of capture.

Several species of squid are, in fact, likely to be encountered in British waters. The Common Squid (*Loligo forbesii*) and the Long-finned Squid (*L. vulgaris*) are two fairly large species which are normally found some distance offshore, attaining a length of up to 2ft. Their distribution range extends up the Atlantic coast of Europe into the English Channel and parts of the North Sea.

In shallow inshore waters, the tiny 2-inch long *Sepiola atlantica* swims over, and burrows into, areas of sandy sea-bed. They are sometimes brought ashore in seine nets, and make an excellent bait for cod, bass and many other predatory fish when presented whole on the hook.

There is also another excellent type of small squid, about 5 inches long, which is imported frozen from North America, primarily for human consumption. Often referred to as Californian Squid, packs of these frozen squid are obtainable from a few coastal tackle shops, as well as from fishmongers in towns with a large immigrant population.

The Common Cuttlefish (*Sepia officinalis*) attains a length of about 12 inches, and is basically very similar to its close relatives, the squids. The main points of difference are a broader and somewhat flattened body, and a continuous fringe of paired fins extending from behind the head to the tip of the body.

Although not regarded quite so highly for bait as

squid, pieces of cuttle tentacle and flesh nevertheless make a very acceptable offering for black bream, bass, pollack and many other kinds of sea fish. The head, when presented on leger tackle, also makes a good bait for conger or large ground-feeding bass.

When boat fishing it is not at all unusual to come across dead cuttlefish floating on the surface of the sea, surrounded by a flock of herring gulls pecking at the corpses. One widely held theory is that these cuttlefish have been killed by ship's propellers. Be that as it may, these floating cuttlefish are well worth salvaging for use as bait, provided the gulls have not already pecked away too much of the flesh.

Catching Squid and Cuttlefish

My introduction to the art of catching cuttlefish on rod and line happened by chance many years ago while a friend and I were driftlining for bass in Portland Harbour, near the mouth of the Fleet backwater. For bait we were using tiny live pollack, fished on a flowing trace about two feet off the bottom.

Before long we began to get a constant succession of vigorous plucking bites, but no matter how quickly we struck at these bites we failed to drive the hook home. Then in desperation I tried a slow, gentle retrieve – and up to the surface came a large cuttlefish, its beaked mouth still sunk into the neck of my tiny pollack. Its method of attack put me in mind of a stoat sucking the blood of a rabbit.

The landing net was slipped under the cuttlefish, which promptly let go of its prey and discharged a cloud of ink. With the cuttle still in the net, we splashed it around vigorously for a few more seconds to make it use up all its sticky, unpleasant-smelling ink; then swung it aboard.

The shoal of cuttlefish continued to attack our baits for another hour or more, and by the end of that time we had boated several dozen. These were later cut up for bait and salted down – this being long before the days of domestic deep-freezers.

Shallow water squid can also be caught by the same method, but normally they are encountered well offshore, and unfortunately in deeper water they tend to let go of the bait before they can be brought to the surface and netted. The reason for this, it seems, is that they become disturbed by the rapid increase in light intensity as they are reeled upwards towards the surface.

Over marks where feeding squid are known to concentrate, you can overcome this problem by rigging up one or two large treble hooks immediately below a suitable fish strip bait. The instant you feel a squid biting at the bait you jerk the tackle upwards, and with luck your quarry will be foul-hooked on one of the trebles. It's hardly the most sporting of fishing methods, of course; but after all your main concern is to obtain some fresh bait as quickly as possible, and it is almost impossible to hook a squid fairly in that small beaked mouth.

Baiting Up

First of all, as previously mentioned, a fresh-caught squid must be induced to discharge its supply of ink, and this is done by prodding it with the net or gaff — preferably while it is still a foot or two below the surface.

After killing the squid, slit its body open and remove the internal shell, or 'pen' — so-called because in the case of *Loligo*, it resembles an old-fashioned writing quill. At the same time rinse away any lingering traces of ink and remove the outer skin. This can be peeled or scraped off quite easily.

The head, removed from the body with a sharp knife, makes an excellent bait for conger, cod, bass, ling and — in some areas — thornback rays. The usual method of baiting up is to insert the hook at the severed end so that the point emerges in the centre of the tentacles. Two tentacles can then be snicked over the point and barb to prevent the point from becoming buried in the bait. Some anglers use the two long tentacles for this purpose, but normally I prefer to cut these off and use them separately as bait for smaller species such as black and red bream, whiting, etc. When used in this way the tentacles should be cut into sections about 2 to 3½ inches in length, depending on the size of hook. The piece of tentacle is then threaded up a round-bend, sliced-shank hook, leaving about 1 to 1½ inches hanging free below the bend.

The body, or mantle, of the squid can be cut into tapering strips and presented on a long-shanked, fine-wire hook. The strips can be threaded on the hook in two different ways — the ultimate choice depending on the mood of the fish, and whether or not they are 'biting short'.

Possibly my favourite method is the one recommended elsewhere in this book for fish strip baits, in which the tapered end of the strip is slid up the hook shank and trapped securely alongside the hook-eye by the looped end of the nylon trace. The hook-point is thrust through the strip a second time at a position corresponding with the lower end of the shank, leaving about a third of the bait dangling below the bend of the hook.

In the second method the hook-point is passed through the pointed end of the strip, and then (after twisting the bait) passed through it again. In this method a larger proportion of the bait is left hanging free below the bend. This can be very effective when the fish are biting voraciously, but may result in missed strikes when they happen to be in a finicky mood.

Finally, it is possible to bait up with a whole small squid when fishing for large cod, conger, ling, etc. The neatest and safest way to do this is to use two hooks mounted in tandem fashion. The top hook is threaded

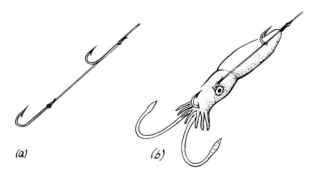

Fig. 43 (a)   Tandem hook tackle for mounting whole small squid; (b) Method of baiting up.

into the flesh at the tail-end of the body for the full length of the shank; after which the point and barb are brought out again through the side. The bottom hook is thrust through the back of the head so that the point emerges among the tentacles. Here again the two long tentacles can be removed and cut up for use separately as baits for smaller species.

Whelks

The Common Whelk (*Buccinum undatum*) has been used as bait for centuries by commercial fishermen when setting longlines for cod, haddock and dogfish. The rod and line angler will find this shellfish equally useful, as it is widely distributed and attains a good size — the shell often measuring up to 3 inches in length.

The whelk's cone-shaped shell, with its well-defined whorls, is too familiar a sight to require more detailed description. Although small whelks are sometimes found in rock pools, those large anough to be used as bait dwell on the sea-bed beyond the low tide line, usually in areas where sand or mud predominates.

On some parts of the coast decent-sized whelks can be caught in drop-nets baited with fish offal, and lowered from deepwater piers and harbour moles. Alternatively, it is often possible to purchase a supply of live whelks from commercial fishermen, who often find quantities of them in their trawl nets and crab pots. They can be kept alive for a day or two if placed in clean hessian sacking that has been well saturated in sea water. Failing that, they can be placed under layers of wet seaweed. They should, of course, be stored in a cool, shady place.

Baiting Up
To extract the whelk from its shell it is necessary to crack open the whorls — taking care at the same time to avoid damaging the flesh inside. This can be done with a hammer or similar 'blunt instrument', although possibly the neatest method is to lay the shell on its side on a

firm surface, and then hit it smartly once or twice with the blunt rear edge of a heavy-bladed Bowie knife, using a chopping motion. This destroys the suction, and the whelk's grip on its shell, and the shellfish can then be withdrawn intact quite easily. Having done this, cut off the horny disc-shaped operculum which was the whelk's protective 'front door' before it was so rudely evicted from its home.

When baiting up with a whole whelk it is best to use a long-shanked, fine-wire hook − preferably one with a round bend. The type known as an 'Aberdeen' hook serves the purpose very well. First insert the point of the hook at the tapered end which originally fitted into the pointed upper end of the shell; then thread the shellfish up the shank and bring the point and barb out through the firmer lower part of the body.

For smaller species of fish, such as red and black bream, wrasse and pouting, one can also cut the whelk into portions and present them on a smaller hook.

In European waters the Common Whelk is encountered in a wide range of depths from shallow water to approaching 50 fathoms. Its distribution range includes the open Atlantic coastlines, the English Channel, North Sea and West Baltic.

Hermit Crabs

The Hermit Crab is not only an excellent sea angling bait; it is also a remarkably interesting little crustacean. The front half of its body is covered with a crusty shell, and is superficially rather like a tiny lobster − although its colour is reddish, whereas the colour of a live lobster is a deep slatey-blue.

The abdomen of the hermit crab, however, is soft-skinned; and in order to protect this very vulnerable part of its anatomy it lives a hermit-like existence in an empty sea shell of the 'corkscrew spiral' type. Tiny hermit crabs usually inhabit periwinkle shells, and these are often found in shallow tide pools, but the larger hermit crabs are mostly encountered beyond the five fathoms line.

As it grows older, and increases in size, the hermit crab finds it necessary to change its small periwinkle shell for a larger whelk shell. This 'house-moving' process is repeated from time to time, until eventually, after perhaps ten years, the fully-grown hermit crab will be occupying the largest whelk shell it can find.

In fact, several species of hermit crab occur in our waters, but the two most commonly used as bait by sea anglers are *Eupagurus bernhardus*, which attains a length of about 4 inches, and the somewhat smaller *E. prideauxi*, with a maximum length of about 2½ inches. Both are found in considerable numbers wherever sea-bed conditions are suitable, and for obvious reasons are often present in areas where whelks are numerous. They have a distribution range which, in European waters, extends from the Mediterranean to the English Channel and North Sea. As a general rule they favour sandy or muddy areas, which may or may not be interspersed with scattered rocks.

Large numbers of hermit crabs are often hauled to the surface by inshore trawlers, and as these small crustaceans have no market value they are usually dumped back over the side again as soon as the net has been emptied. However, for the price of a pint or two, most trawlermen are only too willing to put aside a quantity of hermit crabs for any angler who can arrange to collect them when the vessel returns to harbour.

Because hermit crabs are scavengers, with a special liking for the flesh of dead fish, they also frequently find their way into crab and lobster pots, and in suitable areas are a favourite fishing bait of light-vessel crews, who catch them in baited drop-nets and small-meshed netting traps known as 'crawlie-pots'.

There are small spiny, sickle-shaped hooks at the end of the hermit crab's soft and delicate abdomen, and by means of these the creature anchors itself to the central pillar of the upper shell. This makes it extremely difficult to pull a live and healthy hermit crab from its shell without breaking it; although it does relax its grip when dead or dying. When a freshly-caught hermit crab is to be used for bait, therefore, the simplest method of extracting it is to crack open the spiral whorls of its whelk shell home. This deprives the crab of its anchorage, and allows it to be withdrawn quite easily. Any suitable weapon can be used to crack open the shell, but care must be taken to avoid damaging the delicate bait inside. One simple method is to lay the shell on its side on the bait cutting board, and then hit it firmly with the back edge of a heavy-bladed Bowie knife.

After the hermit crab has been removed you will, more often than not, find that it has been harbouring a 'lodger', in the shape of a large plump ragworm, in the shattered upper whorls of the whelk shell. This type of ragworm (*Nereis fucata*) also makes an excellent bait. Thus the angler who does a deal with a professional fisherman for a supply of hermit crabs will often obtain two baits for the price of one!

Baiting Up

There are two methods of baiting up with hermit crab. For plaice, flounders, dabs and whiting it is best to use the soft abdomen, or tail section, with just a little of the shell-covered thorax attached. You will find that the bait can be cut quite easily at the appropriate spot with a sharp knife. The point of a fine-wire, round-bend hook is then inserted into the severed end, and the tail section threaded round the bend and up the shank until the hook-point emerges at the extreme end of the tail. If necessary, more than one hermit tail can be threaded on to the hook in the same way,

For larger fish, such as cod, bass and rays, the whole hermit crab — minus legs and claws — can be used as bait. In this method a larger hook is passed first through the fleshy abdomen and then a second time through the

Fig. 44   Baiting with hermit crab, using the soft fleshed tail and part of the thorax. (To provide a larger bait, two tails can be threaded on to a long-shanked hook, one above the other).

crusty thorax. This latter method is particularly useful when fishing from a boat or pier, where distance casting is not required.

An Example of Underwater 'Togetherness'

I have already mentioned that the hermit crab shares its shell, and its food, with a ragworm. Quite often, however, the shells occupied by the larger hermit crabs are covered by all sorts of other small sea creatures, such as barnacles, saddle oysters, camouflaging sponges and hydroids, and – most remarkable of all – a beautiful species of sea anemone (*Adamsia palliata*).

This spirit of mutual co-operation between different types of organism is known as symbiosis, and marine biologists often quote the case of the hermit crab and the sea anemone as a classic example. When threatened by some predator the hermit crab retreats into its shell, and the anemone discourages the intruder from making a closer examination with its stinging tentacles. In return the anemone helps itself to fragments of the hermit crab's food.

This particular sea anemone (*A. palliata*) also provides the hermit crab with another important advantage. By wrapping its basal disc right around the crab's whelk shell home, it effectively increases the capacity of the shell, and in this way the crab is saved the problem of finding a larger shell as it grows bigger.

A partnership such as this would be remarkable anywhere in the underwater world. When one of the partners is such a humble, vegetable-like creature as the sea anemone, our feeling of wonderment gives way to one of sheer mystification.

Part Four
Other Baits

Baits for Grey Mullet

Bread, in one form or another, is a favourite bait with expert mullet fishermen. It has the important advantage of being always readily available, and even 'wild' mullet soon acquire a taste for it with the assistance of some bread-based groundbait. Another advantage is that bread has little or no appeal for most other kinds of saltwater fish, so the mullet specialist who uses this bait can rest assured that he will not be pestered by tiny pouting, wrasse and similar unwanted small fry.

Paste

This is possibly the easiest type of bread bait for the beginner to use. It is prepared by cutting a thick slice from a stale white loaf and trimming off the outer layer of crust. The remaining slice of 'crumb' is then wrapped in a square of clean white linen cloth and soaked in water for a few seconds.

On lifting cloth and bread from the water, squeeze out all surplus water and knead the cloth thoroughly between your fingers until the bread inside has been reduced to a stiff paste. Shape the paste into a ball and keep it wrapped in the damp cloth until required for use.

To bait up with paste, take a pinch between your fingers and thumb and mould it around the hook, leaving the hook-point slightly exposed.

Flake

This bait requires no preparation. Simply pinch off a small piece of the white, spongy crumb from the inside of a NEW loaf, and wrap it round the shank and bend of the hook, leaving the point protruding. The secret is to apply the piece of flake so that it folds itself around the hook shank; after which it is pressed into place between forefinger and thumb.

Crust

For this bait you need a loaf about three days old. Slice off a layer of crust from the underside of the loaf about 3/8-inch thick, so that there is a thin layer of crumb attached to the crust. If there is time before you go fishing, dampen this slice of crust slightly and leave it for several hours between two boards with a weight on top. In fact, leave it overnight, if possible.

Next, take a sharp knife and divide the slice of compressed crust into narrow strips; then divide each strip again crossways to form numerous 3/8-inch cubes.

To bait up, insert the hook point into the brown crust side so that it emerges through the thin layer of crumb.

One final word of advice — keep the strips and tiny cubes of crust in a bait box with the lid closed. If left exposed to sun or wind for any length of time they will dry out and become useless.

Additives

Pilchard oil and anchovy paste are sometimes added to the above-mentioned bread baits in the belief that they give them extra 'mullet appeal'. This may well be true, but the additives should only be used in very small quantities.

Cheese is a hook bait that has lured many a big mullet into the landing net. If you use the ordinary cheddar or 'mousetrap' variety, it *must* be fresh and moist, because cheese that has become dried-out and brittle will be useless for your purpose. Even fresh cheese will have to be kneaded thoroughly between the fingers before it can be moulded around the hook.

Processed cheese — the sort sold in small foil-wrapped triangles — is also attractive to mullet, and it is more convenient to use because its creamy consistency makes baiting up a lot easier.

Mullet sometimes become very adept at sucking cheese baits off the hook without falling foul of the barbed point. When this problem arises it is often

97

possible to outwit the mullet by mixing in some strands of cottonwool with the cheese.

Obviously, cheese bears no resemblance to the mullet's natural diet, so it is something of an acquired taste. However, I know of one excellent fishing spot at Dungarvan, on the south coast of Ireland, where the local estuary mullet have become accustomed to feeding on curds and whey flowing from the outfall pipe of the local creamery. John Casey, a well-known Dungarvan angler, began capturing these mullet many years ago on cheese baits; then he adopted the cheese and cottonwool method that I have just described. Finally he discovered that the mullet cruising around the outfall pipe had become so conditioned to swallowing anything small and white that he was able to catch them on a hook baited only with cottonwool!

Banana pith, cut into small cubes and presented on a size 10 hook, can be an excellent mullet bait in some areas. It seems to be particularly effective in certain West Country estuaries.

Macaroni, lightly cooked and cut into tiny pieces suitable for a size 8 or 10 hook, has proved very useful in harbours, and near estuary moorings, where the local mullet shoals have grown accustomed to feeding on galley scraps thrown overboard from yachts.

Beach hoppers are plentiful on most shingle or sandy beaches. There are several species, varying in size from about $\frac{1}{3}$ to ¾-inch, and each favours its own type of habitat. However, those most commonly used as bait for mullet are generally to be found under rotting seaweed along the high tide line. They are often present in their hundreds, and can be trapped quite easily under a child's small-meshed shrimping net. Be sure to keep them in a deep-sided container, otherwise they will hop out again as soon as you take off the lid to bait up.

Incidentally, it is advisable to gather considerably more beach hoppers than you are likely to need for hook bait, and to use the surplus mixed in with the groundbait.

Groundbaiting

Groundbaiting from the Shore

Although most shore anglers go to considerable trouble and expense in their search for bigger and better catches, surprisingly few ever bother to try groundbaiting tactics.

Yet there are many types of shore position, such as steep-to rocks, harbour walls and sheltered coves, which readily lend themselves to this method of attracting fish.

Boat anglers have long appreciated the advantages of groundbaiting when bottom fishing for black bream, rays, skate and conger; and no one is likely to dispute the need to lay down a good rubby-dubby trail when drifting for blue shark.

Shore anglers, however, seem to have a blind spot when it comes to groundbaiting. The one exception is that rather rare and localized character, the mullet specialist. *He* knows only too well that some form of groundbaiting is absolutely essential to get his elusive quarry interested in his hook bait!

Sometimes you will come across a shore fishing position which already has a supply of groundbait 'laid on' — as, for example, when a harbourside fish cannery or packing shed disgorges a constant trickle of fish scraps into the water from a waste pipe.

Normally, however, you will have to provide your own groundbait, and the secret of success is to offer it 'little and often', so that the appetite of the fish is stimulated without being satisfied.

Crushed shore crabs, pieces of fish guts and livers, the minced-up flesh of pilchards, mackerel, herring, sprats and other oily fish — all these make excellent groundbait for most of the species caught from the shore.

Continental sea anglers, unlike their British counterparts, really do appreciate the value of groundbaiting when fishing from rocks or harbour walls. On the Portuguese coast, for example, the local commercial rod and line fishermen (yes, there really are such people!) mostly work in pairs on the Atlantic-pounded rocks. One man, using a long bamboo rod and fixed-spool reel, fishes with float tackle baited

with sardine. His companion concentrates on ground-baiting the swim, and spends all his time flicking small pieces of chopped sardine into the water.

The fish taken in this way consist mainly of bass to 10lb and over, bluefish, grey mullet, various species of bream, John Dory and large mackerel. These anglers are literally fishing for their livelihood, and experience has taught them that groundbaiting is the surest way to obtain a good catch.

Similar tactics pay off just as handsomely when rock fishing around the British Isles – particularly on the steep-to rocks of Devon and Cornwall. Of course, the method of groundbaiting can be varied to suit the coastline and strength of the local tides.

For example, when rock fishing during a rising tide it is often possible to place small heaps of groundbait on those rock ledges which lie fairly close to the water. Thus, as the tide gradually rises, each small pile of groundbait gets washed off the rock in turn.

Needless to say, it is important to place the groundbait on the up-tide side of your fishing position so that it drifts down past the hook bait.

When fishing from an openwork pier or jetty, it is usually best to suspend the groundbait in a small-meshed netting bag. Then stream your tackle from the downtide side of the pier, giving the groundbait bag an occasional shake to release some of its contents.

Beach fishing may not, at first sight, seem to offer much scope for groundbaiting, but if carried out under suitable conditions it is certainly worthwhile. In a sheltered bay or cove it is possible to boost catches of bass, conger and rays by filling an old sack with some mashed-up mackerel or herring, and pegging it out in the shallows at low water.

Even a steeply shelving shingle beach offers possibilities for groundbaiting, as I discovered by chance one summer's evening. I had just returned from a dinghy fishing trip, and after hauling my boat up the beach I

Fig. 45   These two professional Portuguese rock anglers know the value of groundbaiting. While one holds the rod, and reels up the fish that earn them their living, his companion feeds a steady trickle of mashed-up sardines into the swim.

went back to the water's edge and gutted the catch of black bream and pollack.

No sooner had I finished this task when I noticed a shoal of mackerel breaking the surface close inshore. They were still about 200 yards away along the beach, but moving fast in my direction.

I grabbed my spinning rod from the boat and tackled up with a small metal lure. Without moving from that spot I managed to bag over two dozen mackerel, because the fish suddenly slowed down and began milling around when they came to the patch of water where I had recently gutted the fish.

This, of course, was a case of unintentional groundbaiting; but there was a useful lesson to be learned from it!

Groundbaiting from a Boat

When fishing from an anchored boat it is often possible to add considerably to the size and variety of the catch by laying down an attractive trail of groundbait. The method used to achieve this can be varied to suit the fishing technique employed, and the depth at which the hook bait is being fished.

For example, when using float tackle, or an unweighted driftline, in quest of near-surface bass, mackerel and garfish, it is sufficient to chop up a few mackerel into hundreds of tiny pieces, and to trickle a steady stream of these blood-saturated fragments over the side of the boat into the running tide. As the pieces of mackerel drift away astern on the current they will attract fish from a considerable distance down tide.

Although fresh-caught mackerel make the most attractive groundbait, it is also possible to obtain excellent results with mackerel from the deep-freezer after they have been thawed out and pulped up. In fact there is no need to restrict the groundbait recipe to mackerel — chopped-up garfish, sprats, pilchards, herrings and crushed shore crabs are equally effective. Indeed, it always pays to experiment in this matter of groundbaits, and as proof of this I would mention that some of my best float fishing catches have been made when groundbaiting with the heads of boiled prawns that had been left over from the tea table!

When fishing close to the bottom in a fair depth of water it is, of course, necessary to lower the groundbait to the fishing depth in some sort of container. The simplest method is to place the groundbait in a perforated metal canister and tie it to the anchor rope a few feet above the anchor itself.

This usually works well enough in depths of up to ten fathoms, but in deeper water, due to the up-tide slant of the anchor rope and the down-tide slant of the reel line, the groundbait is likely to finish up too far away from the hook bait to be of much use. In fact it may actually attract the fish *away* from the hook bait.

Therefore, when deep-sea bottom fishing, it is best to lower the groundbait to the fishing depth on a separate length of fairly thin codline. Needless to say, the groundbait container will need to be weighted with sufficient lead to overcome the pressure of the tide.

Incidentally, the reason why I recommend using a metal canister is that netting bags and similar alternative containers are liable to be torn to shreds by sharp-toothed congers, tope and dogfish.

Many sea anglers have their own favourite groundbait mixtures, but for summer fishing in waters where mackerel are abundant it is difficult to beat a concentrated offering of minced-up mackerel guts and flesh. Alternatively, when fishing for black bream, a very attractive groundbait can be obtained by soaking bran in commercial grade cod liver oil.

Rubby-Dubby

In order to achieve success when drift-fishing for shark it is essential to lay down a generous and unbroken rubby-dubby trail. The rubby-dubby is usually made by pulping up several dozen mackerel in a bucket or similar container until they are reduced to a porridge-like consistency. Alternatively the mackerel can be put through a large, heavy-duty mincer — in which case you should first remove the head, backbone and fins from each fish.

Freshly caught mackerel produce good results when treated in this way, but some shark boat skippers contend that even better results are obtained by using stale mackerel (one or two days old) which have been

Fig. 46   Mashing up the rubby-dubby.

allowed to become soft fleshed and somewhat 'over-ripe'.

The semi-liquid rubby-dubby is poured into an old onion sack, or small-meshed bag, and then suspended over the side of the drifting boat so that the bag just dips below the surface with the rolling of the boat. Every ten minutes or so the bag should also be shaken and slapped vigorously against the side of the hull for a few seconds so as to clear any meshes which may have become clogged up, and to release an extra thick cloud of fish particles into the water.

Preserved Baits

Deep Freezing

For the sea angler who occasionally returns home with an embarrassingly large catch of prime cod, plaice, whiting, turbot, sea bream or other valuable food fish, a deep-freezer can be a worthwhile investment.

As a bonus, there is also the convenience of being able to keep an emergency supply of deep-frozen bait always on hand, ready for those occasions when it is impossible to obtain fresh baits due to gales, inconvenient tides, or some other reason.

There is no doubt at all that deep-freezing is the simplest and most efficient method of preserving a wide variety of saltwater fishing baits. The smell and taste of the bait do not become tainted, as happens when one uses formalin or other chemical preservatives. Nor is freezing so messy and time-wasting as preserving with salt.

The availability of many baits varies according to the season of the year, or with the ever-changing pattern of spring and neap tides. Therefore, at the risk of stating the obvious, your policy should be to freeze down any surplus baits in times of plenty, for use later on when they are no longer available. Two typical examples are razorfish and sandeels, which on many coasts can only be caught during low spring tides.

Squid are one of the easiest and most useful baits to put down in the deep-freezer. On many parts of the coast they can be obtained in quantity from professional netsmen or trawler crews. For best results, clean the squid thoroughly in sea water, and get them into the freezer with as little delay as possible.

Divide them into convenient sized batches, and pack each batch into a separate airtight plastic bag. Squeeze or suck all the air out of each bag before sealing it with a plastic-covered wire 'twister'. Some people use a plastic drinking straw when sucking out the air, but I prefer to use the hollow plastic outer casing of an old ballpoint pen.

This method of packing should be applied to all types of home-frozen bait, and it serves two important purposes. First of all, excluding the air helps to keep the bait in better conditon – particularly baits like sandeels, which also have some visually attractive properties.

Secondly, it is a means of checking that the plastic bag really is airtight. Never use a punctured bag, because this may allow the contents to taint other food in the freezer intended for human consumption.

Alternatively, you may prefer to order through your fishmonger a pre-frozen 6lb pack of imported Californian squid. Primarily intended for human consumption, these are a fairly small variety of squid with plenty of proven 'fish-appeal'.

As soon as you take delivery of the pre-frozen squid, switch on the quick-freeze compartment of your freezer in order to get the temperature down as low as possible. At the same time, thaw the squid in *cold* water just sufficiently to allow you to separate them. Then dry the squid thoroughly and pack them individually into plastic bags. Seal the bags in the usual way and arrange them in the quick freeze compartment so that each bag is actually touching the side of the freezer. After about twelve hours they can be moved to the main part of the freezer.

Mackerel. During the summer months it is a good idea to freeze down a few dozen mackerel for use as bait in late autumn and winter after the shoals of mackerel have left our coasts. They make a useful standby when nothing better is available, but I am bound to admit that however fresh the mackerel are when they go into the freezer, they come out a rather second-rate bait. True, I have caught plenty of good fish on frozen mackerel, but they were all taken on days when the fish were in a feeding mood, anyway.

Nevertheless, frozen mackerel are very useful when thawed out and mashed up to provide a groundbait for use when rock fishing for mullet, bass, mackerel and garfish, or when boat fishing for black bream and many other species.

Herring stand up to deep-freezing much better than mackerel. They seem to retain their attractiveness to fish; although, as in the case of mackerel, the flesh becomes rather soft after it thaws out. This makes it difficult to keep on the hook when distance casting, but this drawback is not so noticeable when it is only necessary to lob the bait out a short distance from a steeply shelving beach or harbour wall.

When fishing a big frozen herring bait for conger or bass, it is usually best to cut the bait in the round, rather than slice the flesh off the backbone.

Sandeels can be frozen successfully provided they are absolutely fresh when they are put into the freezer. It is best to dip them first in a glycerine and water mixture, and then lay them for a few minutes on a wire griddle to drain. After this they can be placed into small airtight plastic bags, about ten to a bag being a convenient number. Take care to arrange the sandeels so that their slender, delicate bodies are lying straight in the bag — not curved or bent.

Bass will readily go for a frozen sandeel, provided you are not fishing next to an angler who is baiting with fresh-caught sandeel. In this sort of situation the fish will choose the fresh bait every time!

Razorfish are well worth freezing down because they are a first-class bait for bass, cod, flatfish and many other species. The secret is to freeze them while they are still alive. It is not a thing I like doing much, but razorfish frozen after they are dead are not nearly so attractive to fish, and they do not have such a long storage life. Like sandeels, they are best stored in batches of about ten to a bag.

Worm Baits. I suppose ragworms and lugworms are the two baits that the majority of sea anglers would most like to deep-freeze. I tried it once with lugworms, and the result was a horrible gooey mess when the worms thawed out. I haven't pursued the experiment further, due mainly to opposition from my wife!

However, large black lugworm can be kept in good condition for about 14 days by first squeezing out the gut; then rolling the worms in dry newspaper and storing them in a refrigerator — NOT the freezer.

So far as commercially preserved lugworm are concerned, I believe there would be a ready market for dehydrated lug if costs could be kept down to an attractive level. I know from personal experience that they catch fish, having produced small batches of dehydrated lugworms by drying them with the aid of silica gel. Soaked in sea water before use, they plump up and catch fish like a freshly-dug lugworm.

Which is more than can be said for some of those shop-bought packets of preserved lugworms!

Salted Baits

Preserving baits with salt has been practised since time immemorial, but it is not done so much in these days of domestic deep-freezers.

The main snag is that the method is rather troublesome and time-consuming. It entails laying the prepared baits on a generous quantity of coarse salt in a suitable container; and then covering the bait with another layer of salt. This can be repeated until the container is filled with alternate layers of bait and salt.

The salt extracts a great deal of moisture from the bait, and after a day or two it will be necessary to remove the bait and pack it again in a fresh quantity of dry salt. It is best to use a large airtight container because this prevents the salt from extracting moisture from the atmosphere in damp weather. The type of large screw-capped glass jar used in sweet shops is excellent for the purpose.

Mussels, cockles, lugworm and squid are all suitable for salting down, and will keep for up to six months or more if stored in a cool place.

A less troublesome use for salt is to sprinkle it generously overnight on shelled mussels, sprats, mackerel fillets, etc. This is not intended to preserve the baits, but simply makes the flesh firmer so that it stays on the hook better when distance casting.

Other Preserved Baits

One often sees lugworms and ragworms, preserved in formalin or by some other chemical means, offered for sale in small plastic packets. Judging from my own experience, and that of numerous angling acquaintances, I would say that these 'packet baits', as they are often called, have very little appeal to sea fish. This is probably due to the fact that the preservative gives the bait an unnatural smell and taste.

Artificial Lures

In recent years there has been a considerable upsurge of interest among sea anglers in the art of spinning with artificial lures. Certainly it is a most rewarding and exciting branch of our sport, because in the nature of things it is the swiftest and hardest fighting predatory fish which are most likely to attack a moving lure.

Oddly enough, though, it is not always the lure which bears a close resemblance to some natural bait creature that catches the most fish. Instead, it is the 'action' of the lure, as it is retrieved through the water, that decides whether or not it is likely to be a killer.

A good lure should wriggle in a lifelike fishy manner; or twist, dart and flash enticingly; or create interesting vibrations in the water. If it does some, or all, of these things there is an excellent chance that predatory fish will be attracted to the lure, and then be stimulated by its glinting movements into attacking it.

Some fish, such as the mackerel, are so governed by this type of reflex action that they will pursue almost anything that is small and shiny — and they can even be caught on a piece of silver paper wrapped around a hook shank. Other species, however, are much more discerning, and a lure that catches mackerel by the hundred may persistently fail to hoodwink the crafty bass.

If a spinning lure (as distinct from a trolling lure) is to be any use it must also cast well. In this respect a self-weighted lure is preferable to one which requires some up-trace lead to achieve the necessary casting distance. This does not mean that self-weighted lures invariably catch the most fish. Very often they do so by virtue of their excellent casting properties; but on other occasions, when the fish are shy, it may be essential to use a light lure with extra lead up the trace.

In the following pages you will find illustrations of a wide variety of lures, together with information on their main advantages, limitations, methods of presentation, and the sort of sea fish they are most likely to catch.

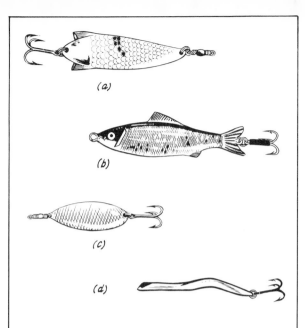

Fig. 47   A selection of self-weighted metal lures
*(a) The Toby wobbling spoon possesses a light fluttering
action. It is an excellent spin-casting bait for bass, and will
also take mackerel and pollack. Available in plain silver
and decorated in a variety of colours; also in various sizes
and weights.*

*(b) Shiny metal fish like this do not possess much built-in
action, but by working the rod-tip during the retrieve
they can be given an attractive 'sink and draw' movement.
Small sizes up to 1oz make ideal mackerel spinning baits;
larger sizes weighing up to 7oz or more can be used to catch
cod and pollack by jigging from a drifting boat.*

*(c) The 'Koster' – an excellent spoon for use in windy
conditions. It possesses an attractive built-in wobbling
action, and has proved itself to be a reliable bass killer. It is
also attractive to mackerel and pollack, and is available in
various sizes and colours.*

*(d) The 'German Sprat' is a traditional design made of
chromed brass, its long, slender shape gives it a superficial
resemblance to a sandeel, and for this reason it can be very
attractive to bass, pollack and mackerel. Smaller sizes,
weighing about 1 oz, are mostly used for spinning, but it is
by working the rod tip important to give the lure an erratic
darting action during the retrieve.*

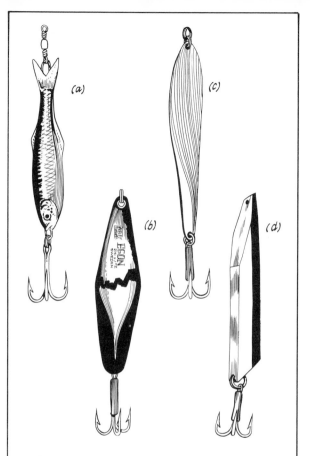

Fig. 48   A selection of cod-jigging pirks of the type which
prove so successful in Scottish sea lochs and Norwegian fjords.
Most of those shown here are available in a variety of sizes and
weights up to 7oz, or 14oz in the case of the 'Egon' (b).
(a) Fish-shaped 'Flashback' pirk
(b) The chromium-plated 'Egon' has a central core of lead
immediately above the hook. This helps to make it sink
quickly – a useful characteristic when fishing in very deep
water.
(c) The 'Lurette' has a curved spoon-handle shape that
gives it a tantalizing fluttering action on the drop.
(d) The 'Sextett' – a cunningly designed pirk which
combines numerous reflective surfaces with an enticing
fluttering action on the drop.

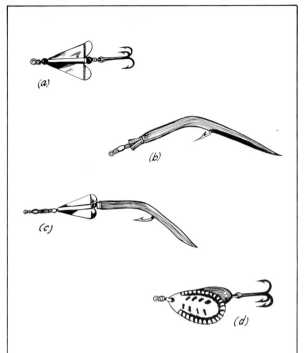

Fig. 49   Various lures
(a) The familiar mackerel spinner has a pair of shiny propeller-like vanes which revolve rapidly as the lure is drawn through the water. Attractive mainly to mackerel and pollack, it is essentially a boat trolling lure. It requires a streamlined up-trace lead, and does not cast well.
(b) The rubber (or plastic) eel comes in a variety of sizes and colours, including fluorescent reds and greens which can be very effective when trolling or spinning for pollack at dusk. To avoid line tangles, this type of lure must be used with an efficient anti-kink lead.
(c) This combination of spinning vane and plastic eel is a deadly lure for pollack, and will also take bass in some areas.
(d) Bar spoon – so-called because the blade revolves rapidly around a central bar of metal as the lure is retrieved through the water. Available in a wide variety of sizes, weights and patterns. Some types are shiny; some are brightly enamelled, and some have fluted blades which allegedly emit attractive underwater vibrations and sound waves. Primarily designed for medium-distance casting with a light spinning rod, bar spoons are capable of catching mackerel, garfish, pollack, coalfish, bass – and even sea-trout in suitable coastal areas.

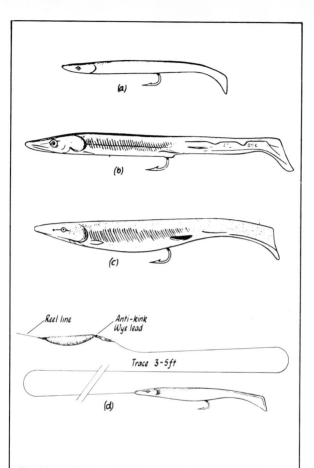

Fig. 50 *Selection of plastic sandeels suitable for light spinning and trolling*

(a) Small 'Red Gill' for inshore pollack, mackerel and bass.

(b) Large 'Red Gill' for offshore pollack and coalfish and bass.

(c) An alternative pattern incorporating some lead ballast in its belly.

(d) Shows method of tackling up with a plastic sandeel when boat trolling, using a large 3 to 4oz Wye anti-kink lead. For casting types (a) and (b) with a spinning rod, the terminal rig is basically similar, except that the trace is shorter and a smaller ¾ or 1oz Wye lead is used. Type (c) which contains some built-in weight, can be cast out without using any up-trace lead.

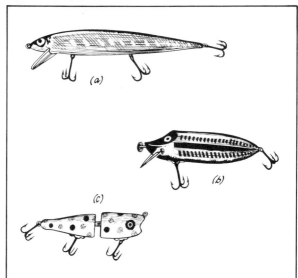

*Fig. 51   Although the majority of plug baits are designed pri-
marily with the freshwater pike fisherman in mind, many of
these lures also produce a ready response from such saltwater
species as bass and pollack. Being self-weighted, plug baits can
be cast with a medium spinning rod without the assitance of
any up-trace lead.*

*(a)   With its slender 'sandeel' shape and lifelike outer skin
of glistening foil, this type of plug can be a real bass killer —
even on those days when the fish refuse to look at any other
sort of artificial lure. Available in various sizes and colours,
with an additional choice of floating or sinking versions.
Judging from our own experience, we would recommend the
slow sinking sort, preferably with dark blue back and silvery
sides and belly*

*(b)   This type of chubby-bodied plug is sold in a bewildering
variety of sizes and colour schemes. Some are made of wood;
others of plastic. Some are buoyant and wriggle along the
surface like a small wounded fish; others sink slowly and
waggle their bodies with a lifelike swimming motion when
retrieved. Some rather expensive ones are fitted with an
adjustable lip which can be pre-set to control the depth of the
retrieve. There is, in fact, infinite scope for experimenting!
However, it can be said that plug fishing in saltwater is most
likely to catch bass in rocky situations, with emphasis on the
big ones.*

*(c)   Jointed plugs also come in a wide variety of sizes and
colours. All the foregoing remarks under (b) also apply to
these lures.*

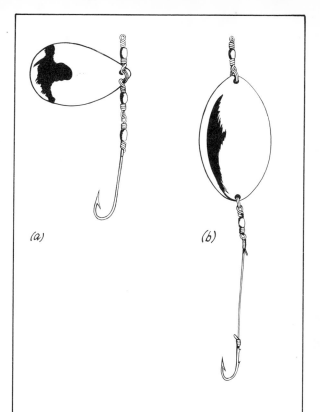

(a)

(b)

*Fig. 52   Lures for baited spoon fishing. The usual choice of
bait with these lures in a medium-sized ragworm, but lugworm,
mussel, cockle and hermit crab tails are also used on some
parts of the coast.*

*(a) This so-called 'flounder spoon' is, in fact, equally attractive
to plaice. It is most commonly used by estuary dinghy anglers,
who troll the baited lure slowly under oar power a foot or two
above the bottom. An alternative method is to suspend the
baited spoon beneath a drifting float. When a flatfish notices
the shiny spoon it swims closer to investigate; then transfers
its attention to the baited hook. This type of baited spoon is
available with either a light celluloid blade or a metal blade.
The celluloid type if favoured mainly by boat anglers, whereas
the additional weight of the metal-bladed type makes it more
suitable for shore casting.*

*(b) The shiny metal blade of this spoon does not revolve.
Instead, it has an attractive fluttering action as it moves
through the water.*

Index